Notorious
TELLURIDE

TALES FROM SAN MIGUEL COUNTY

Broken tracks lead off into the void at the Suffolk Mine above Ophir, Colorado. *Photo by Peter D. Turner.*

Notorious TELLURIDE

TALES FROM SAN MIGUEL COUNTY

CAROL TURNER

Charleston   London

THE
History
PRESS

Published by The History Press
Charleston, SC 29403
www.historypress.net

Copyright © 2010 by Carol Turner
All rights reserved

First published 2010

Manufactured in the United States

ISBN 978.1.60949.086.7

Library of Congress Cataloging-in-Publication Data
Turner, Carol.
Notorius Telluride : wicked tales from San Miguel County / Carol Turner.
p. cm.
Includes bibliographical references.
ISBN 978-1-60949-086-7
1. Frontier and pioneer life--Colorado--Telluride--Anecdotes. 2. Frontier and pioneer
life--Colorado--San Miguel County--Anecdotes. 3. Outlaws--Colorado--Telluride--
Biography--Anecdotes. 4. Outlaws--Colorado--San Miguel County--Biography--Anecdotes.
5. Crime--Colorado--Telluride--History--Anecdotes. 6. Crime--Colorado--San Miguel
County--History--Anecdotes. 7. Telluride (Colo.)--History--Anecdotes. 8. San Miguel
County (Colo.)--History--Anecdotes. 9. Telluride (Colo.)--Biography--Anecdotes. 10. San
Miguel County (Colo.)--Biography--Anecdotes. I. Title.
F784.T44T8 2010
978.8'23--dc22
2010042767

For Charlie

CONTENTS

ACKNOWLEDGEMENTS

Many thanks to the folks at the Colorado State Archives, Colorado Historic Newspapers Collection and the Denver Public Library for their assistance. Thanks also to Peter D. Turner, Richard and Joss Turner, John and Lynn Turner and Jolie Gallagher. I offer a grateful and admiring nod to MaryJoy Martin for her exhaustive research on the Telluride mine labor wars at the turn of the last century and her book, *The Corpse on Boomerang Road*. In the case of the labor troubles, because certain editors were so deeply involved in the action themselves, the local newspapers had become "unreliable witnesses."

INTRODUCTION

On the surface, the story of Telluride and San Miguel County's settlement by the white man is mostly about mining and ranching. Many of these people were courageous, hardworking immigrants; others were rugged "native-born" Americans. Along with the regular folk came a stream of gamblers, "sporting women," thieves, addicts, con artists, killers, obsessives, megalomaniacs, idealists and ghost chasers—not to mention the gullible, desperate and a few pure innocents.

These are the stories of those "not-regular" folks, primarily as recorded—and sometimes embellished—by the newspapers of the day. The events described here took place not just in Telluride but across the entire county—from the Disappointment Valley in the west to Norwood, Placerville, Ophir and up among the treacherous cliffs and peaks of the San Juans.

WANTED DEAD OR ALIVE: JESSE MUNN

Born in 1882, Jesse R. Munn was an ambitious lad from the rugged ranchlands of southwest Colorado. A hardworking and "well known miner and prospector,"[1] when he came into town he drank a lot and found companionship among Telluride's many "sporting women." He also tended to carry a gun, but he had no trouble with the law until what seemed like a minor brush in April 1910. On that fateful occasion, Telluride night marshal Arthur Goeglein arrested Munn and threw him in jail for a night, charging him with carrying a concealed weapon. A few months later, Munn's resentment over this incident would lead to a much more serious encounter between the two men.

Munn's mother and stepfather, Mr. and Mrs. Sam H. Thompson, were prominent citizens who lived on the Thompson Ranch north of Durango until they sold it in 1906. Sam Thompson had been county commissioner of La Plata County for several years. Munn's biological father was "said to have been killed in Durango, years ago, in some sort of trouble and his mother later married Thompson."[2] Jesse had a brother, R.D. Munn, also of Durango.

Perhaps using capital from his parents, Munn invested in several mining ventures. Between 1905 and 1908, he worked a lease on the Alta Mine with partners, including Telluride town treasurer V.U. Rodgers. Later, he traveled to New Mexico, Nevada and Texas in search of mine properties. In 1909, Munn and a partner, Joe King, leased the Summit Mine, located on the ridge between Gold King Basin and Ophir. There, Munn worked as a foreman over as many as forty men.[3]

Despite these accomplishments, Munn was headed for big trouble. On Saturday night, July 30, 1910, Munn and a friend, Dick Martin, headed into Telluride from their home near Ophir. They spent the evening at a bordello called the Cosy Corner on Pacific Avenue. About 1:30 in the morning, the two men headed to the Pick and Gad Saloon on Pine Street, accompanied by three Cosy Corner prostitutes—Ella Morrison, Beatrice Earl and Pearl Elliot. While the group was in the Pick and Gad, Night Marshal Goeglein came in and briefly joined them but soon went on his way without any trouble. A while later, the group returned to the Cosy Corner's barroom. Soon, Goeglein entered the place and asked Munn to step outside with him. They headed out the front door, and moments later, five shots rang out.

The others ran outside and found Goeglein on the ground with Munn standing over him. People from the street also converged on the scene. A man named Bill Jenkins was nearby at the time and witnessed Munn's last two shots. As Jenkins ran toward the prone figure, he saw Dick Martin come out and urge Munn down Pacific Avenue, telling him, "Come on, get out of this."[4]

> *When he [Jenkins] arrived he placed his arm under Goeglein's head and raised him up asking who had shot him. His lips barely moved and his eyes stared. He was practically dead. Just then, Jim Steel, assistant night marshal came up and assisted Jenkins to carry Goeglein to the sidewalk. They asked the girls for a pillow which was brought and placed under Goeglein's head. Dr. Hadley than [sic] came and said the man was dead.[5]*

Jenkins stated that as they moved Goeglein's body, his gun fell out of its holster. They checked and found that all the chambers were full. They concluded that all five shots had been fired by Munn, with three of those going wild. Goeglein had a bullet wound in his right cheek and another in the middle of his left shoulder blade—in his back. The doctor said either of the injuries would have been fatal.

An hour later, authorities located Dick Martin in bed at a place called Jim Spellman's. "He appeared to be maudlin drunk but the officers believe this was feigned. He was locked up and is in the county jail. The three girls who were in the Cosy Corner at the time were also taken into custody but later released. They will be kept handy for witnesses, however."[6] Jesse Munn was nowhere to be found.

The coroner's inquest was held Wednesday, August 3. Another witness, Leon Edwards, testified that he'd been standing outside by another bordello called the Big Swede's half a block away when he heard the shots. As he ran down the street, he passed two men hurrying away into the night.

The doctor testified that a bullet had entered Goeglein's right cheek, traveled through his head and lodged under the skin at the back of his skull. "The other entered from behind over the middle of the left shoulder blade going forward and upward to the right passing through the left pleura cavity cutting the large blood vessels at the base of the heart, the bullet finally lodging in the lower part of the neck. This wound was sufficient to cause practically instant death."[7]

The women of Cosy Corner testified that the shooting started almost instantaneously as the men left through the door. One of the women, Beatrice Earl, said, "No one else could have done the shooting other than Jesse Munn."[8]

The coroner's jury ruled that Goeglein's death had been caused by gunshots fired by Jesse R. Munn with felonious intent. After the inquest, the sheriff released Dick Martin, Beatrice Earl, Ella Morrison and Pearl Elliot.

Authorities in nearby towns were quickly notified about the fugitive, especially those in the Durango area, where his mother, Mrs. Thompson, was said to be nearly hysterical with anxiety over her son. A number of posses set out to scour the mountains. They printed "Wanted Dead or Alive" posters, offering a $1,500 reward for Jesse.

A local mortician prepared the body of Arthur Goeglein, and numerous friends and sympathetic citizens escorted the casket to the train depot. Arthur's cousin, Telluride water commissioner A.J. Goeglein, traveled with the body back to the family home in Fort Wayne, Indiana. There, Arthur's grieving family awaited him, including his father, stepmother and several brothers and sisters. In Telluride, Arthur had been a very popular young man who had just been elected to membership in the Elks Club. He had only been in town for about a year.

There was much angry talk in town and threats of lynching, especially because it appeared that Munn may have shot the marshal in the back without warning.

In the following weeks, Munn sightings abounded—most of them false. One week after the killing, a credible report came in that Munn had been spotted near Little Cone, south of Placerville. A ranch woman named Mrs. W.F. Cooley spotted a heavily armed man opening a gate on a trail while his fatigued horse waited. When he noticed her, he rode away. Another nearby ranchman named Coffman gave food and hay to a stranger on a horse. Mr. Coffman noticed the fellow had several gold teeth, which matched the description of Jesse Munn. These ranch folk later visited the post office in Placerville, where they first heard about the murder and the reward.

Despite these sightings, an entire month dragged by without further word about Munn. Rumors circulated that friends of his must be hiding him in the mountains near Telluride.

Finally, on September 16, nearly six weeks after the shooting, word arrived that Jesse Munn had surrendered to a New Mexico ranch hand named Meyers, dubbed "Broomtail" in the papers. Munn had reportedly turned his horse loose and walked right up to Broomtail, who worked at the Wright Ranch, five miles east of Farmington.

San Miguel County sheriff George Tallman and Undersheriff C.C. Hicks headed down to New Mexico and picked up the fugitive. They put Munn in a car and drove all night long back to Durango. After resting a day, they brought him back on the train to Telluride, where a curious and irate crowd awaited them at the train depot. Tallman, however, had anticipated a mob scene and had left the train with his prisoner a mile below town, where a rig met them and drove them quietly into town without being seen.

The *San Miguel Examiner* admitted that had Jesse been caught right after the shooting, he would have "stretched hemp." However, the only thing the good folks of Telluride wanted now was a fair trial and a healthy dose of justice.[9]

Papers reported that the ranch hand Broomtail would collect the generous reward but that certain New Mexico law enforcement officials also tried to claim the money. Telluride authorities later refused to pay the reward to anyone, saying that no one had earned it because Munn had surrendered.

When the sheriff brought Munn in, he also re-arrested Dick Martin, Ella Morrison, Beatrice Earl and Pearl Elliot, holding them as witnesses. Tallman soon released the women on "appearance bond" but kept Martin in jail.

The story soon filtered out that Munn had first fled to Placerville, then Utah and then Gallup, New Mexico. He had also spent time hiding in a canyon in the eastern part of San Miguel County and had later ridden his horse to exhaustion and become lost. He claimed he had intended to turn himself in all along but was waiting for the mob fervor to die down.

Munn's parents hired two prominent Durango attorneys to represent him—B.B. Russell and Willis A. Reese. Munn was arraigned in mid-November, at which time he pleaded not guilty. His defense was that he had thought Goeglein was pulling out his gun to shoot him but that he managed to shoot first. He said he never meant to flee from justice but felt that he would be lynched if he stayed in town.

About the same time as Munn's surrender, a mysterious female witness entered the picture. She had reportedly come to Telluride from Glenwood Springs to spy on her lover, who she believed was in town for an illicit tryst. While creeping through Telluride's alleys and back streets looking for her paramour, she had witnessed the entire shooting. One version of the story said she left town without contacting authorities but told a friend, who let the story out. Another story said she contacted the deputy district attorney before leaving Telluride and that he told her to keep quiet for the time being.

In the third week of November, Munn's attorneys applied for a change of venue. Judge Shackleford agreed that so much prejudice existed against Munn in San Miguel County that he would never get a fair trial. The *Telluride Journal* reported on itself, paraphrasing the defense assertion that most of this prejudice had been created and promoted by the *Telluride Journal*. Judge Shackleford ordered the trial moved to Ouray, to commence the first week of December.

This created a wave of excitement in Ouray, as the Munn case was big news in the region. The *Ouray Plaindealer* declared that it was "one of the most sensational and one of the hardest fought murder trials ever held in Western Colorado."[10]

On the morning of Saturday, December 3, 1910, Sheriff Tallman took his prisoner over to Ouray, and they began the process of seating the jury from a pool of Ouray County citizens. The jury consisted of "O.P. Lyons, J.W. Martin, Gus Mose, W.S. Rose, W.C. Davis, R.W. McKean, John Wooten, Frank H. Miner, J. Larson, E.E. Barnes, Gus Arps, O.L. Howell."[11]

The trial began the following Tuesday, with the prosecution represented by District Attorney R.M. Logan of Delta, Deputy District Attorney L.W. Allen of Telluride and Deputy District Attorney Wheeler of Ouray County. Jesse Munn's brother and stepfather attended the trial.

Jesse was described by the *Plaindealer* as "a young man of rather attractive appearance. He appeared in court neatly dressed. During the trial he seemed to be cool and calm, occasionally consulting his attorneys and tak[ing] a quiet but nevertheless keen interest in every proceeding."[12]

In his opening remarks, Defense Attorney Russell said that Goeglein was a "tremendous big fellow"[13] who liked to throw his weight around as night marshal, "keeping himself in the limelight by his bullying and brutality."[14] Russell said that Goeglein hated Jesse Munn and had previously threatened his life. He said Munn carried a gun because he'd also been threatened by a notorious Italian named Tony Sardini, who was rumored to be a member of the Black Hand mafia. Munn had been shift boss at the Butterfly Terrible Mine, and Sardini and others working there had reportedly beaten him up after a disagreement. Munn also had problems with a former Telluride policeman named Lou Miller—enough so that he felt he needed to carry a weapon.

The prosecution presented a number of witnesses who painted a picture of Munn as someone who carried a gun and regularly got into trouble in the red-light district, including an incident when Munn "got into a quarrel with a colored piano player at the Idle Hour, and shot up the place."[15] Witnesses insisted that Goeglein had no grudge against Munn but that Goeglein had warned him about his behavior and gun packing. They told the jury about the incident the previous April when Goeglein and another officer had arrested Munn for carrying a weapon and made him spend a night in jail.

Testifying about the night of the shooting, Beatrice Earl said they'd all had eight or nine beers during the early part of the evening and then went to the Cosmopolitan Café for supper. They later visited two more saloons—the Idle Hour and the Pick and Gad—where she said they drank eight or ten more beers. While they were at the Pick and Gad, Marshal Goeglein came in and, at Miss Earl's invitation, sat with them for a time and smoked a cigar. After Goeglein left, the group returned to the Cosy Corner and drank more beer. At that time, she testified, Goeglein came into the Cosy Corner, stood by the slot machine and then spoke to Munn, saying, "Come out, Jess. I want to speak to you a minute."[16] Munn finished his drink and then followed Goeglein out the door about six feet behind the marshal.

> As Munn went out of the door it swung to behind him, and was within a few inches of being closed when the fatal shots were heard. Beatrice Earl said that there were five shots fired, three in rapid succession, a short interval and then two more shots. As the shots were fired, Martin pushed the door shut.
>
> Miss Earl was not sure which of the girls reached the door first, but thought that she and Pearl Elliott reached it about the same time. As she opened the door and looked out, Munn was standing by the door, and falling or staggering. Goeglein was trying to rise from the ground, and was falling into the street. A moment later she looked and saw two colored men and Jim Steele bending over the body of Goeglein. She thought that a colored man named Jenkins was the first man to reach Goeglein, with policeman Steele arriving a second later.
>
> On being cross examined, Miss Earl stated that no gun had been displayed during the evening and that absolutely the only unpleasantness

was Martin's refusal to let her buy Goeglein a cigar with his (Martin's) money at the Pick and Gad.[17]

The two other Cosy Corner ladies gave similar testimony, saying there'd been no trouble that evening but only "a great deal of good natured joshing."[18]

The curious crowds at the trial were soon craning their necks to get a look at the next witness—the mystery woman from Glenwood. Her sensational history quickly became a story in its own right. Kathryn Taylor was described as "aged 27 years, attractive and very bright and quick witted."[19] The details of her life quickly mesmerized every person in the courtroom:

> *Her home is in Glenwood where she, by her own admission, manages a house of ill fame. She formerly lived in New York City, was educated in eastern schools, claims to be of good family and declared to The Plaindealer that when about 22 years of age began her life of immorality.*
>
> *The sensational report came from Denver that this young woman was badly wanted at the time of the famous trial as a witness in the celebrated Thaw murder case.*
>
> *Kathryn admits that she knew Harry Thaw, that she and some other girls were engaged in revels with him in New York City and Atlantic City prior to the murder of* [Stanford] *White but she was in Washington, D.C. when the murder was committed. Hearing that they were to be subpoenaed as witnesses she and her girl companions fled to the west. She was in Denver for awhile, later in Glenwood. She refuses to divulge of what nature her testimony would have been had she appeared in the Thaw trial. She says that trial is over and she has no desire to gain any notoriety connected with it.*[20]

The 1906 murder of the famous Manhattan architect Stanford White by the wealthy and troubled Harry Thaw in New York City was the most sensational case of the period. Kathryn Taylor was said to be a friend of Evelyn Nesbit, the woman at the center of the case.

As for her role in the Goeglein murder case, Taylor's testimony stunned the courtroom: she stated emphatically that she had witnessed the entire event and that, without warning, Munn had shot the marshal in the back.

She explained that she had traveled to Telluride in search of a man named Joe Leek (or Teak), who, she said, was "drunk in Telluride" while carrying a good deal of money. She said she had gone there to rescue him. She had found him and made plans to meet for dinner that night, but Leek did not show up. She ran into Marshal Goeglein, who agreed to help her find the fickle fellow. She and Goeglein were cruising from saloon to saloon, looking for Leek, when they approached the Cosy Corner. Goeglein told her to wait for him on the corner, saying, "I want to see a man here." She waited about fourteen feet from the front door while Goeglein went inside, coming back out a few seconds later. She had a clear view of the scene, as it was illuminated by an electric streetlight. Munn was about three feet behind Goeglein as they came out the front, and as Munn reached the door, he fired into Goeglein's back. Goeglein threw up his hands, and she could see he was not holding a weapon. She said she heard three shots as she ran away in terror.

When Defense Attorney Russell cross-examined her, observers noted a great deal of hostility between the two. Under questioning, she admitted that she had been running a "sporting house" in Glenwood Springs for the past year and a half. She denied that Joe Leek was her lover and insisted that she was looking for him on behalf of an alderman in Denver. The alderman had accused her of stealing Leek's money and causing his "disappearance," so she was trying to clear her name by finding him and sending him back to Denver.

As it turned out, Mr. Russell had approached Miss Taylor before the trial, trying to find out what her testimony was going to be. He now pressed her to say why she had previously refused to tell him, and she declared that she had promised not to talk about the case. Once again, she created a stir in the courtroom when she announced that Russell had tried to bribe her to give him her story. She denied Russell's suggestion that the prosecution had paid her to testify.

The defense next attempted to cast doubt on the notion that Munn had shot Goeglein in the back. When Russell quizzed Dr. Hadley, the doctor admitted he could not say which of the two bullets had entered Goeglein's body first—the one in his face or the one that entered his back.

The first bit of information that resembled a motive emerged when a Dr. M. Rothwell testified that he had encountered Munn the previous April, right after Munn had been arrested for carrying a concealed weapon. Munn had been kept in jail all night without bail. Rothwell said Munn was irate about the incident and had sworn at the time, "They will never take another gun away from me."[21] Another witness gave similar testimony, but it was stricken from the record and the jury was instructed to ignore it.

On Thursday and Friday, when the defense presented its case, Jesse Munn took the stand. He said that, as he followed Goeglein out the door, Goeglein made a move as though to draw his gun and Munn drew first and shot him in the face. As Goeglein turned, Munn shot him again in the side or the back, and when the officer was down and trying to stagger to his feet, Munn shot twice more. He denied shooting Goeglein first in the back. He said he feared Goeglein was going to kill him and claimed that Goeglein had told him he would kill him if he caught him with a gun again.

Munn's friend Dick Martin testified on his behalf. Admitting that he'd had about fifteen drinks that night, he claimed that Goeglein had wanted to kill both Munn and himself. When Goeglein beckoned Munn outside, he followed Munn to the door and stood holding it for a moment. He saw Goeglein turn around and put his hand on his gun. Goeglein had partially pulled it out when Munn shot him. Martin then slammed the door shut and returned to the bar. When the shooting stopped, Munn came to the door and told him, "I did not mean to do it."[22] Martin admitted that he told Munn he should get out of town but insisted that he did so only because he believed Munn would be lynched.

The defense called another witness—a woman named May Erwin who lived in one of the "cribs" across the street from the Cosy Corner. May said she had seen four people come out of the Idle Hour a while before the shooting. Later, as she was taking her hair down, she went to the window and looked out. She "saw the flash of gun, and saw Goeglein shot in the face. The second shot was then fired, which seemed to hit Goeglein in the shoulder."[23] She saw Munn and Martin running away up the street but did not see Kathryn Taylor. Upon cross-examination, Deputy District Attorney Allen quizzed her about why she had not told them any of this information, and she declared flatly that the other girls who had talked to Allen had been abused and got into a lot of trouble. When he asked which girls had been abused, she said,

> *"I was abused, thrown in jail and treated badly."*
> *She said that when she met Russell, she thought he would protect her and therefore told him her story. Allen asked if the story was in payment for this protection. An objection raised did not permit the witness to answer this question.*[24]

In fact, the three "sporting women" had been arrested twice—first right after the shooting and again when Munn turned himself in.

In rebuttal to May Erwin's testimony, the prosecution put Sheriff Tallman on the stand, who testified that when he first interviewed May, she told him she'd been in bed during the shooting and did not get up to look until it was over.

A "sporting woman," May Erwin, saw Jesse Munn shoot Marshal Goeglein from the window of one of the "cribs" in Telluride's red-light district. *Drawing by Richard Turner.*

It came out during the trial that Munn had purchased the murder weapon, a Colt .41, at the Tomkins-Cristy hardware store the day before the shooting. Officials believed he had purchased it for the express purpose of shooting Arthur Goeglein, though they presented no evidence to support that. The *Plaindealer* described the weapon in almost loving detail as

> *single action blue steel and beautifully finished. The balance is excellent and the action as smooth as that of any gun ever made. The trigger is practically set at a hair, being so gentle that a babe could discharge the gun without disturbing the aim. No more effective instrument for Munn's purpose could have been found. The large calibre, the soft-nosed bullets, in fact every feature of the occurance [sic], indicate the purpose for which the weapon was purchased, and added to the fact that immediately after the murder Munn hid the gun; show that its object had been accomplished.*[25]

After the shooting, Munn had stashed the gun in the Anderson livery stable in Telluride. Law enforcement later searched the stable and uncovered the weapon. Marshal George Hall reportedly kept it as a souvenir.

Late on Friday, the case went to the jury. On Saturday night, after ten hours of deliberation, the jury reached a verdict. Many observers were shocked and indignant when the jury announced that they'd found Jesse R. Munn guilty of voluntary manslaughter. Most criticized the sentence as too light. The *Ouray Herald* wrote: "Jesse Munn was a bad man, and it was shown in the testimony that he was a dangerous man. He was violating the law by carrying a concealed weapon, and the fact of his having the gun was evidence that he was not a law abiding citizen."[26]

Before pronouncing sentence, an obviously disgusted Judge Shackleford delivered a lecture to Munn that was aimed more at the jury:

> *You have been tried by a jury which has brought in a verdict which to my mind, is inexplicable. The jury should have returned a verdict against you of some higher degree of homicide or acquitted you.*
>
> *The evidence in this case shows that you took the life of the marshal of Telluride when he was in the discharge of his duties and that you shot him in the back. It convinces me of your guilt and, to my mind, a jury that returns a verdict of this kind holds human life very cheaply. It is difficult to get men to perform the duties as marshal, especially in this part of the country.*
>
> *However, I have to abide by the verdict of the jury.*[27]

Judge Shackleford gave Jesse Munn a sentence of seven and a half to eight years of hard labor in the state penitentiary. Munn's family and friends celebrated this verdict, having feared he would hang.

Expressing outrage at the verdict, the *San Miguel Examiner* compared it with another case, providing a vivid example of imbalance in the system of justice:

> *All things considered, that verdict is absolutely the worst of all the bad ones that San Miguel county has had anything to do with, and they have had several in past years.*
>
> *Compare these two results:*
>
> *Harry Voris stole a can of lunch tongue and got from two to four years in the penitentiary.*
>
> *Jesse Munn deliberately murdered Arthur Goeglein by shooting him in the back after having made threats against him and planned to kill him, and the jury in the case made it impossible for the sitting judge to give the murderer over seven and one-half years in the same institution.*[28]

Jesse Munn was quickly escorted to Cañon City to begin serving his sentence. A few days later, the *Telluride Journal* gleefully reported:

> *As "chambermaid of the pen" Jesse R. Munn will enjoy the New Year's festivities tomorrow. From an outdoor life, care free and victim of*

A promising young man, Jesse Munn's ego got the better of him. *Colorado State Archives.*

wanderlust, the change from the New Year's of 1910, is a hard blow to the slayer of the night marshal of Telluride. Born and bred in the broad open of the mountains, a wanderer when the wish overtook him, care free and reckless in temperament, never having been subjected to control, either of the law or his own will, the day will not be a happy one to the new inmate of the state prison.

Jesse Munn is known no longer. His identity is now concealed under the designation of Convict No. 7945, and he is but an infinitesimal atom in the mills of the Colorado penal system. Assigned to duty as "chambermaid" in one of the prison dormitories, his duties are not difficult nor ardous [sic], but prove much harder for him than would employment in the open air which he has always known.[29]

Shortly after the trial, Munn's friend and aide, Dick Martin, was briefly arrested once again—this time for accessory after the fact, on the grounds that he had helped Munn escape. These charges were later dropped.

In prison, Munn quickly earned status as a trusty. He soon found himself back "in the broad open of the mountains," living in a road camp in Larimer County. About a year into his sentence, he was working with a road gang at Pingree Hill near Red Feather Lakes, west of Fort Collins. On January 14, 1912, along with a fellow prisoner named Joe Mattocks, Jesse escaped.

```
7945-JESSE R. MUNN
Received Dec 15th 1910.From Ouray County 7 1/2 to 8 years

for Murder. Age 27. Weight 145. Height 5-9-1/2.

Complexion Light. Bust 36. Waist 35 3/4. Thigh 19 3/4.

Neck 15. Hat 7 1/8. Shoes 7.Hair and Eyes Brown.

Build medium. Trade Miner &Tool sharpener.

Small scars over right eye and nose.Small mole on right
shoulder. Vaccination mark on Left arm.Blotch on right
hip. Hair on body below waist. Teeth 4 kxxx gode others
bad.
```

Munn's Record of Convict. *Colorado State Archives.*

Deputy Sheriff Cook of Fort Collins and a Wyoming farmer named A.C. Cornilson tracked the fugitives and closed in on them about a week later near the Wyoming-Colorado border. Some papers said the men were found holed up in a cabin near the town of Tie Siding, Wyoming. Reports on the incident vary, but the bare facts are that Mattocks gave himself up and went peacefully back to Cañon City. Jesse Munn resisted arrest, and Deputy Sheriff Cook shot and killed him. When killed, Munn had been in the process of weaving himself a blanket against the cold Wyoming winter.

Authorities sent Jesse's body back to his parents in Durango, where he was buried at Greenmount cemetery.

In June 1912, the Durango law firm of Russell and Reese sued Munn's parents, the Thompsons, for unpaid attorneys fees in the matter of *The People v. Jesse Munn.*

Postscript: In March 1911, the "mystery witness" of the Munn case, Kathryn Taylor, was once again in the news. The *Telluride Journal* published this notice, taken from the *Denver Post:*

> *Katharyn* [sic] *Taylor, "the woman in white" of the notorious Thaw case, again figures in a tragedy of life and death—this time in Glenwood Springs, Colo., where last week, a young son of a wealthy and prominent family of Roanoke, Va., committed suicide on her account. Spurned by this beauty of the half-world, Edwin Woolfolk, 27 years of age, drank chloral hydrate and expired in the rear room of the Silver club saloon.*[30]

DEATH IN THE DISAPPOINTMENT VALLEY

Sometimes a story emerges from the pages of history and proves that life does imitate art. The saga of the Nash, Dunham and Estes families of Disappointment Valley possesses all the love, betrayal, devotion and tragic death of a Shakespearean tragedy.

In 1879, a small party of explorers headed by Wilson "Wilks" Nash entered the Disappointment Valley in the western portion of today's San Miguel County. They were looking for an unspoiled area where they could raise cattle, and they found it. Although the area was known to be a Ute hunting ground, Nash brought his wife, Mary Ann, and their four children, and they settled on a homestead and went to work building up their herd. Thirteen years old when they arrived, their eldest son, James "Jim" Nash, would become one of the Disappointment Valley's most prominent and controversial citizens.

Around the same age as Jim Nash, a boy named Jack Dunham also grew up in the valley and ran cattle. Dunham was quieter than the rowdy and charming Jim Nash. Both men would eventually die a violent death over the love of the same woman.

Another important family in the region was the Estes family. Back in 1859, Joel Estes had been one of the first pioneers to enter what today is Rocky Mountain National Park. The town of Estes Park is named after him. Several years later, Estes moved his family west to the Dolores area, a journey that killed his first wife, Martha. He later married again, but his children considered the new stepmother to be cruel, and they got away as quickly as they could.

Scrub, arid plateaus and the big sky of the Disappointment Valley in western San Miguel County. *Photo by the author.*

In January 1888, the oldest Estes daughter, Lena, married Jack Dunham. Lena was a beautiful woman with a dark intense gaze, a temper and a mind of her own. In December of that same year, she objected vigorously when her younger sister, Tennie, suddenly announced that she was going to marry the carousing, womanizing Jim Nash. Like her sister, Tennie was a pretty girl but had a gentler nature than Lena. Still, she had made up her mind, and Lena was unable to stop the marriage.

Despite a certain competitiveness between the couples, the two men rode the range together. Jack and Lena Dunham had two children; Jim and Tennie Nash had three. As the years passed, the Nash herd grew considerably larger than the Dunhams', and the common wisdom among range folk was that Lena envied the wealth enjoyed by her younger sister.

On October 11, 1901, Jim and Tennie were struck by tragedy when their ten-year-old son Lee suffocated to death when a creek-side cave collapsed on him.

Meanwhile, Jack Dunham had developed rheumatism and was increasingly unable to keep up with his ranch work. Soon, he could no longer ride the range. Lena Dunham, who reportedly hated housework, put her six-year-old daughter, Laura May, to work in the kitchen and took over her husband's job. By all accounts, Lena's proficiency on a horse and running livestock was as good or better than most men.

Soon, gossip about Lena Dunham and Jim Nash flourished in the Disappointment Valley cow camps. Tennie, still grieving over the loss of her son, dismissed the rumors.

On September 25, 1904, Jim and Lena rode into the Dunham ranch house after a day rounding up cattle. Soon after Nash entered the house, he and Dunham had an argument. On that day, Jim Nash shot and killed Jack Dunham.

Conflicting stories circulated about what really happened in the Dunham ranch house. According to newspaper accounts, Lena Dunham headed into the kitchen to prepare dinner, and Nash followed her, playing with his niece in the kitchen. Jack Dunham was stretched out on the lounge in the front room. According to Nash, Dunham suddenly appeared in the kitchen doorway, waving a knife and cursing at Nash, telling him to "hit the road." Nash said he pulled his gun to keep Dunham away and backed out of the door. Dunham then ran to the barn and got his revolver. He ran after Nash, who had mounted up and was headed home. Nash turned and shot Dunham

Jim Nash shot Jack Dunham at Dunham's ranch property. *Drawing by Richard Turner.*

in the head. He shot him twice more in the chest before Dunham dropped dead in the dirt.

Nash turned himself in to authorities in Rico, telling them that Dunham had often been depressed about his situation and jealous of the amount of time Lena spent with Nash out on the range. He was arrested for the shooting and went on trial in October 1904. He pleaded justifiable homicide on the grounds of self-defense. The jury failed to come to a verdict, with eight of the jurors voting for acquittal. With that, the prosecutor entered a *nolle prosequi*, which means they declined to proceed with further prosecution. Jim Nash went home a free man.

It wasn't long after the trial that Lena Dunham moved into the Nash homestead. Rumors instantly circulated across the desert landscape that Jim Nash had divorced Tennie and married her sister Lena. Other salacious stories described the threesome living together in a bigamist relationship. Later on, it came out that immediately after Nash shot Dunham, Tennie Nash had left her home and moved in with her brother, William "Wid" Estes. She obtained a divorce from her husband in May 1905.

In the fall of 1905, a year after killing her husband, Jim Nash married the widow Lena Dunham in New Mexico.

Not surprisingly, Jack and Lena Dunham's fourteen-year-old son, Irving "Honey" Dunham, had difficulties adjusting to the idea of his mother marrying the man who had killed his father. From that day on, bad blood existed between stepson and stepfather, and Honey Dunham never stopped believing that Nash had murdered his father.

About a year and a half later, Jim Nash was arrested once again. This time, Wid Estes rode into Rico and swore out an arrest warrant for Nash, charging that Nash had beat up his first wife, Tennie, with a six-shooter.

Lena accompanied her new husband to jail in Rico. He was charged with assault with intent to kill Tennie Nash. Lena paid his bond, and the couple left.

Nash's story differed considerably from that of Wid Estes. Nash claimed he was asleep in bed when he was urged to get up and go to a dance. When he arrived, a brawl arose. Nash said he was under attack, and he lashed out at everyone in his path. Tennie just happened to be at the wrong spot at the wrong time. He said he was convinced that he'd been lured there so his enemies could kill him.

Nash did not serve any time for the assault.

Jim and Lena continued living and ranching together, growing wealthier. Jim possessed enough charm that many folks still grudgingly liked him, but the iron-willed Lena was less popular. Some said it was her conniving that ultimately resulted in the death of Jack Dunham. Lena's daughter, Laura May Dunham, lived with them until she married in 1907 at age sixteen. That same year, Lena bore Jim a son, Alvin Nash, and they eventually moved to Farmington, New Mexico. In 1911, Tennie married Henry. L. Ellermeyer.

In 1910, stepbrothers Earl Nash—the surviving son of Jim and Tennie—and Honey Dunham lived together, working as stock ranchers near Dolores, Colorado. Early on, Honey Dunham showed signs of being disturbed, getting into repeated scrapes with the law. Lena always came to his rescue, much to the disgust of Jim Nash, who felt she indulged her son. In March 1909, Honey was arrested at Norwood for forgery but got off without a prison sentence. In October 1911, he married Cordelia McDermott, and the couple eventually had three children.

On June 12, 1914, another tragic event struck this star-crossed family. Twenty-year-old Earl Nash was living in a cow camp on the Nash ranch. As an adolescent—before Jack Dunham's death—Earl had ridden the range with his father and Lena Dunham. For the past year or so, young Earl had often made "jokes" about how he was going to kill himself. On this occasion, he rode into the camp, dismounted and handed his horse over to a friend. To another man in camp he gave his bridle, and to another he gave his dog. Next, Earl Nash drew his revolver and shot himself in the eye.

His stunned comrades could do nothing to help him, and he died early the next morning. Friends and family claimed it wasn't suicide, that he had merely slipped while performing his "stock joke," a theory that ignored the fact that he gave his belongings away before pulling the trigger. Others were simply mystified by the act, pointing out that his father was wealthy and that Earl, therefore, had no reason to kill himself.

Yet another tragedy struck when Lena's half brother, Cleve "Unk" Estes, shot a local cowboy during an argument in 1916. Cleve spent the rest of his life in prison and mental institutions.

In late April 1922, the sins of James Nash finally came home. Now in his sixties, Nash was on a cattle drive in Utah with his stepson, Honey. One night, the men were playing cards in a cabin on Montezuma Creek when an argument erupted. Honey Dunham drew a gun and shot Jim Nash dead. Newspaper reports said that Nash's body, riddled with bullets, was taken in a wagon to Dolores, where he was laid to rest.

The general consensus was that Honey Dunham finally had his revenge for the murder of his father.

In May, Honey had his preliminary hearing. The single eyewitness to the shooting was a man named Rex Perkins. He testified that Nash had made threats against Dunham and ordered him out of the region. Another man present in the cabin had slept through the entire event.

The judge charged Dunham with voluntary manslaughter instead of first-degree murder, setting his bond at $2,500. As she had been doing for years, Honey's mother and two-time widow, Lena Nash, provided security to the bondsmen.

Later that year, in November, the involuntary manslaughter charge was dismissed, but Honey was once again arrested on a charge of first-degree murder.

In April 1923, Honey Dunham went on trial for the murder of his stepfather. Many family members, including Lena, attended the trial in a show of support for Honey. After a large number of witnesses testified, the jury went out for eighteen hours and returned with a verdict of "not guilty." Honey Dunham was set free.

Despite his lucky escape, Honey Dunham set out on a path of self-destruction, only in a different manner from that of his stepbrother, Earl

Irving "Honey" Dunham, who never accepted that his mother married the man who shot his father, finally had his revenge. *Colorado State Archives.*

Nash. In June 1923, thirty-year-old Dunham was arrested in Cortez for stealing tires. Lena Nash spent all afternoon at the jail, but he had no other visitors. That night he escaped, apparently with assistance from friends on the outside who sawed through the outer bars of his cell and gave Dunham a gun, which he held on his cell mates while he crawled out. His friends then whisked him away in a Buick automobile. Officers from Colorado, New Mexico, Arizona and Utah joined the chase. He was quickly caught in Moab by officials who held him for Colorado authorities to come and fetch him.

Dunham pleaded guilty, paid a fine and promised to leave Montezuma County. However, his criminal career was just getting started. In 1933, Dunham was sentenced to two and a half to seven years for running a confidence game. He was paroled after about two years but was returned to prison after violating his parole in 1937. He was discharged in 1938.

In 1941, Dunham was back in prison on another charge of running a con game. In 1950, he was charged with forgery, and again on the same charges in 1955. His last stint in prison lasted one year, and he was released in 1957. His prison record states that Irving "Honey" Dunham had an eighth-grade education.

THE HIGHGRADER AND
RATTLESNAKE LIZ

Highgrading was a common crime back in the day, and many more probably got away with it than were caught. The process was simple. A miner casually left work at the end of each shift with a few chunks of ore in his pockets. Over the weeks and months, the chunks added up and could yield a tidy amount of gold, silver or other precious metal. For those who worked in a mill, highgrading could be even more lucrative because they had access to the powdered concentrate created when the ore is crushed and chemically processed.

Late in the summer of 1910, Will L. Erwin was working as an amalgamator's assistant at the Liberty Bell gold mine above Telluride. He was twenty-eight years old, described as a "high-minded" lad and beyond reproach, "about as innocent looking a thief as ever came down the pike."[31] He had enjoyed an excellent reputation as a trusted employee at the Liberty Bell for several years. For a short period, he left to work at Goldfield near Cripple Creek but came back to Telluride and resumed his old position. After he returned, his employers noticed a change in his behavior and slowly grew suspicious. They began to watch him.

On August 23, 1910, Erwin left for another of his frequent "vacations." The folks at the Liberty Bell were convinced he was up to something and asked for help from law enforcement. First, Erwin traveled to Salt Lake City and then to Chicago. It wasn't clear whether he was followed on the entire trip, but upon his return about ten days later, his movements were being observed by Telluride marshal Robinson and his men.

When Erwin's train arrived at Placerville, he was accompanied by a mysterious woman, who got off the train there. The couple said their

Ruins of the Liberty Bell Mine. *U.S. Geological Survey Photographic Library.*

goodbyes on the platform, and then he handed her a package before getting back on the train to Telluride. His "watchers" separated then—some staying in Placerville to watch the woman and some following Erwin to Telluride.

When Erwin arrived back in town, he went to a boardinghouse, where someone tipped him off that he was being watched. He slipped out the back of the building and headed along the river out of town, but he was apprehended by Telluride law enforcement and hauled back into the station. When they searched him, they found $480 on his person. In his trunk, they discovered a collection of empty bands that banks use to package currency. This disclosure later led to some speculation around town that Erwin may have buried most of the loot.

After unsuccessfully trying to bribe the marshal, Erwin wrote out a ten-page confession. It turned out that when he left for his vacation, he was carrying with him 1,200 ounces of amalgam, which he took to Salt Lake City and sold for cash. He admitted that it was not his first sales trip to Utah. He'd been highgrading at the expense of the Liberty Bell for almost a year, for a total take of well over $10,000. Depending on the method used in the calculation, that amounts to anywhere between $233,000 and $4.3 million in today's dollars.[32]

His alleged partner in crime, the mystery woman, was known in Telluride as Mrs. Kennedy. Erwin, also known as Mr. Kennedy to a local hotelkeeper, had taken a couple of prior vacations with his "wife" at the Telluride hotel.

Meanwhile, the next morning in Placerville, Erwin's mistress got on the stage to Paradox Valley. She was followed. She was the lone passenger as the stage traveled from Redvale to Naturita. Suddenly, the stage was hailed by a man on a horse. She screamed that there was a holdup, but the "bandit" turned out to be Deputy Sheriff Jack Rose, who informed her that he was taking her back to Norwood.

There, he escorted her to the Western Hotel, where he temporarily deputized the two lady proprietors—Miss Ida McCall and Miss Mabel Biddle. The two innkeepers quickly searched the prisoner, coming up with $2,700 from among her things. The deputy guessed that this wad of money was the package Erwin had handed her on the station platform at Placerville.

The mystery woman had a couple of other names besides Mrs. Kennedy. Some folks knew her as Mrs. Anna Wells, who lived with her brother on the Wiggins ranch on Cottonwood Creek, twelve miles from Nucla.[33] Though she was known in Placerville as Mrs. Kennedy, some aspects of her behavior there had earned her a nickname that residents used behind her back— Rattlesnake Liz.

After a night at the Western Hotel, guarded by Deputy Rose and a local man named Eugene Galloway, Rattlesnake Liz was brought back to Telluride to join her partner in facing charges of highgrading.

In mid-November, Will Erwin was arraigned and pleaded guilty to theft of $10,000. He was sentenced to three to five years in the penitentiary. His confession must have exonerated his mistress, because Rattlesnake Liz was allowed to go free—albeit without the $2,700. When asked what he had done with the rest of the money, Erwin claimed he had lost most of it—about $6,000—when he left it on a streetcar in Chicago.

THE TROUBLED SAGA OF THE SMUGGLER-UNION MINE

O n the night of November 19, 1902, Arthur Lancelot Collins, manager of the Smuggler-Union, was passing a quiet evening in the mine office up in Marshall Basin, playing cards with friends. Outside in the dark, a shot rang out. A window shattered, and thirty-four-year-old Arthur Collins fell forward, his back riddled with buckshot.

The story behind the shooting of Arthur Collins interweaves with the story of Telluride itself. The Smuggler-Union Mine, incorporated in 1891, was one of the biggest employers in the region. Originally managed by a popular local man named Nate Mansfield, the mine operated for years with little trouble. Miners, most of whom were foreigners, earned three dollars for an eight-hour day and held union meetings on the premises.

In 1899, an out-of-state conglomerate called the New England Exploration Company purchased the Smuggler-Union. One of the new owners sent his twenty-seven-year-old son-in-law, Bulkeley Wells, to oversee the transition. Wells would later become a pivotal character in the history of Telluride, but for the moment, he showed up for a few days, announced a change in management and left town again.

The new manager, Arthur Collins, instituted a slew of new policies that angered the miners' union, known as Local 63. He introduced the fathom, or contract, system, which paid miners by the fathom (six cubic feet) instead of a daily wage. On the fathom system, if a miner was working a good stope, he could earn more than three dollars a day; otherwise, he could end up in debt to the company, a situation in which more than a few found themselves. Collins also gradually decreased the pay for a fathom from twenty-six dollars

Right: Mining ore out of a tunnel was difficult, backbreaking labor. *Library of Congress, Prints & Photographs Division*.

Below: A view of Marshall Basin, home of the Smuggler-Union Mine. *U.S. Geological Survey Photographic Library*.

to as little as fourteen dollars. At the same time, he increased the amount miners had to pay for tools and powder. He fired muckers, who broke and shoveled the ore. Miners now had to muck their own ore, which drastically increased the amount of work they had to do for the same pay. Workers also discovered that they had to board at the Smuggler-Union boardinghouse or else they found themselves unemployed.[34]

Collins also signaled his attitude toward the union by announcing that Local 63 could no longer hold its meetings on Smuggler property. The group moved to the Jupiter Mine, whose owner, John E. Conn, was more sympathetic.

Collins wasn't finished. He replaced union shift bosses with nonunion men and installed family members in top positions. He also developed a reputation for exploiting ethnic tensions in order to create divisions among the Finnish, Swedish, Tyrolean, Austrian and Italian miners.

In short, for those working at the Smuggler-Union, life went downhill fast after the takeover.

The members of Local 63 fought back. In September 1900, they elected a new leader, someone they believed would stand up to Collins. Vincent St. John had moved to Telluride in 1897 at the age of twenty. Though very young, he was popular, fair-minded, determined and nonviolent.

St. John asked Collins to either restore the three-dollar daily wage or provide a three-dollar minimum income for contractors. Collins said no. He made no effort to conceal his opinion that those who didn't make money on the fathom system were lazy and incompetent and that the union was full of "foreign born half wits."[35]

St. John did not want a strike, so he offered a compromise—a miner would work for ten days to prove himself, and then he could get on the guaranteed three-dollars-per-day plan. Collins still refused.

It wasn't long before town leaders began taking sides in the battle— particularly Telluride's two newspapers. Francis E. Curry, editor of the *Telluride Journal*, was anti-union, while Charles Sumner of the *San Miguel Examiner* was pro-union. These two men and their newspapers quickly became major players in the growing dispute.

On May 1, 1901, about a year after the takeover, 350 Smuggler-Union miners walked off the job. Foremost among their demands was a return to the way things were before: three-dollar pay for an eight-hour day. Vincent St. John promised a peaceful strike, but Collins didn't believe him and quickly stocked up on arms and ammunition. He hired U.S.-born cowboys from western San Miguel County to guard the mine buildings from strikers, again exploiting the distrust and hatred many "native Americans" had for foreigners.

While Curry of the *Journal* did his best to discredit St. John, Sumner of the *Examiner* published stories of various miners who had been ripped off by Smuggler management.

St. John proposed they submit their dispute to the State Board of Arbitration, saying the union would abide by their decision. Collins, whose pride prevented him from being "managed" by union demands, again said no.

While work at the mine dwindled to a skeleton crew, on May 17, St. John was elected union president for the entire district, which comprised eleven locals, including Telluride Local 63.

On June 17, the Smuggler-Union reopened with fifty "scab" laborers. Strangely, Collins paid these men a flat wage of three dollars a day, which is what the union men were striking for. Strikers were furious, but St. John tried to keep them calm, warning that any violence would only bring in the state militia.

One of the nonunion laborers was a carpenter named William Barney, who was hired to build ore chutes but ended up working as a guard. A loner from out of town, Barney left the property on Saturday, June 22, and headed down into Telluride. The following Monday, he didn't come back. Rumors quickly sprang up that he had been murdered by strikers. Telluride marshal McIntosh figured Barney had simply left town, but Curry thought otherwise. On June 29, he put the disappearance of Barney in a two-column story on the front page, with an insinuating headline: "A MYSTERIOUS DISAPPEARANCE— W.J. Barney, a Smuggler-Union Employee, Drops out of Sight and Hints of Foul Play Are Freely Made."[36]

The situation exploded on July 3, 1901, when strikers confronted a group of nonunion workers at the Sheridan crosscut mine, which was part of the Smuggler complex. Within moments, a storm of bullets fired by mine guards ended the life of a Finnish union miner, John Barthell. The result was a full-scale riot and gun battle, in which two more men died—a deputized worker named Ben Burnham and a mule packer named Joseph Lujan. Several others were injured.

When union workers at the Tomboy and Liberty Bell Mines heard what was going on, they rushed over to join their comrades in the battle. Vincent St. John was roused from bed in Telluride. He and mine manager Edgar Collins, Arthur's more cooperative brother, galloped up the trail through flying bullets. Sheriff Downtain called in the National Guard to round up the strikers, but State Senator William S. Buckley in Telluride successfully urged Governor Orman to hold off.

St. John and Edgar Collins called for a truce. They agreed that all work at the mine would cease for three days and the violence would stop. However, St. John was unable to prevent a mob of angry union men from rounding up the Smuggler-Union guards and scabs and force-marching them over Imogene Pass toward Ouray, telling them not to come back. Later, some of the exiled men described their terror that they were going to be murdered in the alpine wilderness.

Not surprisingly, conflicting stories circulated about who shot first. A huge funeral was held for John Barthell. St. John gave a rousing speech, an event that marked the real beginning of his illustrious career as a charismatic labor leader. A memorial to Barthell and the miners was later erected at the Lone Tree Cemetery.

Though Arthur Collins refused at first to budge, Colorado lieutenant governor Coates finally informed him that the governor was not going to send troops just to enforce the Smuggler-Union's desire to operate with nonunion men. On July 6, 1901, the strike was settled. The parties agreed to a three-dollar minimum pay per eight-hour shift, once a miner had proven himself for a thirty-day period, and the right for the union to meet on Smuggler-Union property.

For those in the union, Vincent St. John was a hero for having negotiated what they considered an acceptable settlement while avoiding further violence. Once the strike was over, St. John focused his efforts on building a union hospital and meeting hall in Telluride.

However, St. John was not a hero to Arthur Collins and his supporters, and they vowed to get rid of the union. They continued spreading rumors and insinuations about the disappearance of William Barney and another local man named John Mahoney who had also disappeared. The *Telluride Journal* promoted these stories despite two critical facts: Barney and Mahoney were not dead. Mahoney, who habitually walked out on his wife Mary and their children, soon surfaced in Salida. As for Barney, St. John finally got fed up with the rumors and hired a detective, who found the man with little effort. It turned out that Barney had moved to Telluride from Nevada only for the purpose of establishing residency in Colorado; he wanted to divorce his adulterous wife without his Nevada neighbors hearing about it. He arrived in Telluride in March 1900 and, after the required year, filed his divorce petition. A few months later, he left town, having been uninvolved in the labor troubles. A year after that, he returned for his divorce hearing, which occurred on April 4, 1902.[37]

It's unknown why those involved in the hearing did not speak up and dispute the *Telluride Journal*'s string of stories about Barney's "murder."

Meanwhile, a Pinkerton detective named James McParland approached Bulkeley Wells. McParland was famous for breaking the Molly Maguires in Pennsylvania, and Wells eagerly hired him to help break the power of St. John and Local 63.

Just before dawn on November 20, 1901, the troubled Smuggler-Union was hit by another tragedy when a fire began in the tram house. The building was located about two hundred feet from the mouth of the mine. About one hundred men were inside the tunnel, which quickly began sucking in smoke. Manager Edgar Collins sent someone in to get the men out, but smoke was already filling the passageways. Efforts to douse the fire failed because the water pipes were frozen. They tried blowing up the tram house, but these efforts also failed. Finally, an experienced man named McKenzie intervened, blowing up a bundle of dynamite at the mouth of the tunnel in an effort to close it off. Unfortunately, the tunnel still wasn't completely sealed, and smoke continued going into the mine.

Twenty-four men died inside the tunnels from smoke inhalation.

That winter, in response to a union boycott of the *Telluride Journal*, several prominent men formed the Telluride Businessmen's Association to fight the union. Members included Arthur Collins; local banker and businessman

View overlooking the Smuggler-Union complex in 1895. *U.S. Geological Survey Photographic Library*.

Addison Wrench; Charles Painter, owner of the *Telluride Journal*; and F.E. Curry, editor of the *Telluride Journal*. Two dozen other anti-union merchants joined. The group hired several "enforcers," in the form of Walt Kenley, a tough Delta County cowboy with a reputation for violence; and two Wyoming gunmen, Bob Meldrum and Willard Runnels. Telluride sheriff Cal Rutan deputized these men, and they lived in the sheriff's quarters, though their salaries were paid by the Mine Operators' Association.

The first week of October 1902, the same week that Vincent St. John celebrated his marriage to Clara Meadows, the union opened the Miners' Union Hospital. The hospital represented a significant improvement in living standards for miners, whose difficult jobs came with a high rate of accidents and illnesses.

Only a few weeks after this landmark event, someone crept through the darkness of Marshall Basin with a shotgun, approached the Smuggler-Union office, spotted Arthur Collins through the window and shot him in the back.

Seven buckshots entered Collins's body, causing profuse bleeding. Several of those entered his kidneys, liver and stomach. While Collins clung to life, a specially commissioned train left Denver carrying Mrs. Collins, Smuggler-Union officials and several surgeons.

The miners' union hall and hospital as it looks today, at the corner of Pine and Columbia in Telluride. *Photo by the author.*

Not surprisingly, attention focused on the union, with the *Telluride Journal* leading the charge with warnings about the "Apparent Transfer of Molly Maguire Headquarters to this District."[38]

Two men returning to Marshall Basin from Telluride that night reported hearing a shot and then encountering a stranger coming down the road at Pandora. They said he had something slung across his back that could have been a rifle or shotgun and that he moved aside as they drew near.

Two days later, on November 21, Arthur Lancelot Collins died.

As the investigation into Collins's murder got underway, his boss, Bulkeley Wells, came to Telluride and announced that he would run the Smuggler Mine himself. Although it had been closed temporarily because of the murder, Wells reopened the mine on December 17.

On December 15, after much political squabbling, a Telluride grand jury handed down a packet of indictments related to the gun battle of July 1901. The indictments included an arrest warrant for Vincent St. John on charges of murdering Ben Burnham, one of those killed during the battle. St. John was not even on scene when Burnham was killed. Several Telluride businessmen immediately posted his bond. A dozen other men were also arrested, while another dozen or so named in the indictments had left town since 1901.

During the May court term, all the indictments against St. John and the others were dropped. However, this was the end of the line for St. John in Telluride; he had been receiving death threats, and the union decided to move him to Denver for his own safety.

The following summer of 1903, Charles Sumner, another of the union's most vocal advocates, decided he'd had enough. He sold the *San Miguel Examiner* and left town.

On September 1, 1903, as part of a statewide rise in labor unrest, Telluride faced another devastating strike—this time by millworkers, who had not been part of the settlement of 1901. Foremost among their demands was an eight-hour workday. Several mines soon closed because the ore couldn't be processed. Cooks and waiters at mine boardinghouses then joined the strike, shutting down two more mines. Within a short time, the Liberty Bell, Tomboy, Nellie, Smuggler-Union and Alta Mines closed.[39]

Although negotiators reached an agreement in Denver during meetings in October, Western Federation of Miners (WFM) leader Bill Haywood later said that the settlement was sabotaged by the Telluride Businessmen's Association.[40]

As the strike dragged on into November, a few minor altercations occurred, but things were mostly quiet. Nevertheless, Colorado's new anti-union governor, James H. Peabody, finally buckled under pressure from anti-

The Smuggler mill, near Pandora. *Drawing by Richard Turner.*

union factions and sent Colorado National Guard troops to Telluride on November 20. Rumors circulated that the troops' salaries were being paid by the Telluride Businessmen's Association and its newly formed iteration, the Telluride Citizens Alliance.[41]

Although State Senator Buckley argued that the strike was peaceful so far, the governor declared martial law in San Miguel County on January 3, 1904. Troops closed saloons, arrested union leaders, evicted union men from Telluride as troublemakers and confiscated firearms from those they did not consider to be law-abiding citizens. They arrested strikers under a vagrancy law and ordered them to either go back to work or get out of town. Many of the deportees, whose families remained at home in Telluride, were taken in by a good Samaritan, Mrs. Kittie Heit. Fondly called "Aunt Kittie," she ran the St. Elmo Hotel in Ouray.

By February 21, 1904, Bulkeley Wells had created a local anti-union militia called Troop A. When the date drew near for the withdrawal of the Colorado National Guard a couple months later, martial law was still in effect in Telluride. Amid rumors that deported miners were planning to return as soon as the guard left, the guard handed military control to Troop A and Bulkeley Wells.

Smuggler manager Bulkeley Wells built this house for himself at the top of Bridalveil Falls. *Photo by Peter D. Turner.*

Wells quickly settled in for a full-scale abuse of power. He censored the papers, telegraph and telephone. He closed the Cosmopolitan Saloon and deported the owners for feeding union miners. He continued arresting strikers on vagrancy charges.

Finally, Governor Peabody revoked martial law March 11, and Troop A was dismissed. As deported union miners began returning home, members of the Citizens' Alliance armed themselves and geared up for a confrontation.

A few days later, on a cold winter's night, Deputy Sheriff Walt Kenley led men from the Citizens' Alliance and remnants of Troop A on a rampage through town. They forced their way into the homes of union miners who had just returned and pulled them from their beds.

A.H. Floaten, a longtime Telluride citizen and union miner, described what happened to him that night when Kenley and his men banged on his door with the butts of their guns, breaking a glass panel. It was bedtime, and Floaten was partly undressed and shoeless. As the men forced their way in, demanding to know who was in the house, Floaten hid in a closet. Kenley found him and jabbed a revolver in his face.

He and his companion pushed me out of the bedroom into the hall. I asked him to let me put my shoes on. Then without warning he struck me over the head with a revolver, cutting a gash about an inch deep in the left side of my head, at the same time telling me that I did not need any shoes. They then pushed me out onto the sidewalk, and my wife came out after them, begging to let me put on my shoes and hat. She had my shoes and hat in her hand, but they would not allow me to put them on. Just as my wife was trying to give me my shoes someone in the crowd, which had gathered, struck me on the head again with a gun. Kenley then took me by the arm and marched me up the alley from my house to a vacant lot near the city hall. The ground was frozen with mud and ice, and my feet were bleeding before I had taken a dozen steps. I was being pushed by one man and then another.

Before we had gone a block we came to a large pool of water in the alley, and someone in the crowd yelled: "Shove the — through the water!" which Kenley did. When we got to the first street I asked them to let me walk on the sidewalk, but they continued down the alley. At this time Kenley was walking directly behind me.

Again without warning he struck me on the head with a revolver, and at the same time someone yelled: "Shoot him!" with an oath. When we got to the vacant lot near the city hall I found that there were a number of others there in almost my predicament. We were surrounded by armed men, some having guns, some revolvers and some both. We were forced to remain there until midnight. Then we were taken to an empty store room, where we were kept until 1:30 a.m. By this time over sixty men had been gathered there, and we were all marched to the depot, where a special train was waiting for us. As I entered the car, bleeding profusely, with my head tied up in handkerchiefs, someone shouted: "If that fellow tied up in white ever comes back to this town he will be hung."

When the train started a fusillade of about 200 shots was fired by the mob as a parting salute. Fifteen members of the mob accompanied us to Ridgeway, forty-five miles out, where we were ordered to get off the train. Fifty-three of us then walked from Ridgeway to Ouray, a distance of eleven miles, where we arrived at 6 o'clock in the morning. The other men remained at Ridgeway, being unable to continue on the journey.

There is but one reason why I did not defend my family and my home, and that is because of the union rule which was laid down at the beginning of the strike, to the effect that we must submit and not resist, so as to give them no excuse to do violence. There has not been one cent's worth of property destroyed during this strike.[42]

Governor Peabody ignored all protests about this illegal and violent roundup. There was no help from local law enforcement, as Sheriff Rutan was a member of the Citizens' Alliance. Union lawyers managed to get a restraining order against Troop A, but after this episode, a good number of the miners and their families gave up on Telluride and left town for good.

At the same time, a rumor began to circulate that St. John was returning to town. The Citizens' Alliance and Mine Operators' Association, insisting that the union intended to go on a rampage, asked once again for help from Governor Peabody, who readily complied. Troop A went back into service and the National Guard returned, with its new commander, General Sherman Bell, famously using the Sheridan Hotel as his headquarters. On March 23, Governor Peabody declared Telluride in a state of insurrection, and martial law was back.

When District Court Judge Stevens came to town for the next court session, he was greeted by armed troops who had been told by Curry that the train was also loaded with union agitators. Stevens was so shocked and annoyed at the martial state of affairs that he announced in an eloquent speech that he was canceling the court session because he could not conduct a proper court in a military state.

Although the strike continued, on June 15, 1904, Governor Peabody revoked martial law once more. However, Wells and Troop A continued rounding up and deporting any union men they could find. On July 1, 1904, Wells shut down the Smuggler because he couldn't keep it staffed.

Finally, in November, the managers agreed to the union demand for an eight-hour day for the millworkers and set a standard scale of wages; this action ended the strike. Wells insisted he wasn't caving to the union but simply did so because the Colorado state legislature was about to enact new wage laws anyway.

Although the strike was settled, much damage had been done to the town of Telluride. During the period of martial law, from the fall of 1903 to the end of 1904, over two hundred people were exiled from Telluride at the behest of the Smuggler Mine management and their supporters. Two hundred more left the area on their own. Before the mine labor wars ended, over seven hundred miners had left the region.

The Citizens' Alliance stayed intact and kept its pet gunmen, Meldrum and Runnels, on staff, sending them after union men whenever they could find an excuse. Runnels landed himself the job of city marshal, while Meldrum became a guard at the Tomboy Mine.

In 1905, Wells had to give up his Troop A, but he had developed a taste for military command. On April 5, 1905, when General Bell resigned from the Colorado National Guard, Bulkeley Wells took his job.

Faraway events next played a role in the Smuggler and Telluride drama. On December 30, 1905, former Idaho governor Frank Steunenberg was blown up by an assassin's bomb. The case was given to Pinkerton agent McParland (previously hired by Wells to break Local 63), who quickly arrested an unstable, pompous fellow named Harry Orchard. Under interrogation by McParland, Orchard came up with an impressive array of confessions that solved just about every crime McParland could think of, including the Telluride murder of Arthur Collins and the supposed "murder" of William Barney. Orchard said that WFM leaders, in particular Vincent St. John, had hired him and a man named Steve Adams to kill the men.

McParland got hold of Steve Adams and went to work on him. Soon, Adams confessed that St. John had hired him to kill Arthur Collins and also to move William Barney's body from one burial spot in the mountains to another.

Since leaving Telluride under threat of assassination, Vincent St. John had remained in hiding in Denver for a time and was then reassigned by the union to Idaho. There, he had aggravated mine owners across the region by organizing unions. He was still receiving death threats telling him to stay away from Telluride. On February 18, 1906, based on the testimony of Steve Adams, the Burke, Idaho sheriff and his deputies burst into St. John's home and dragged him off to jail in Boise. General Wells and his hired sidekick, Bob Meldrum, arrested several other union leaders named by Adams— William "Big Bill" Haywood, Charles Moyer and George Pettibone.

The charges against St. John were soon dismissed, and Haywood and the others were acquitted the following year. In fact, the arrest and trial of these men was a farce. Steve Adams eventually wrote a statement saying that his entire "confession" was fabricated by McParland and Harry Orchard and that he had been threatened with hanging if he didn't sign.

In the wee hours of March 28, 1908, an explosion jolted people awake at the Smuggler-Union complex. When night watchmen hurried to find out what it was, they found Bulkeley Wells out in the snow in his pajamas. He said his bed in the manager's house had blown up with him in it. Wells had a few cuts and bruises but was otherwise unhurt. He claimed he'd been blasted up to the ceiling and thrown across the room, but observers were puzzled by his lack of injuries. Whispers circulated that it was a poorly executed hoax perpetrated by Wells himself in another attempt to cast suspicions on the union.

In July 1908, nearly six years after the murder, Steve Adams went on trial for killing Arthur Collins. The bulk of the case against him was his confession, which he had now refuted. The defense presented an array of witnesses, including a stenographer who corroborated Adams's story that McParland had dictated what to confess.

Mary Mahoney, the wife of one of the "murdered men," had since divorced the husband who had abandoned her and married a local man named Con Meenan. Mrs. Meenan testified that Steve Adams had been at her boardinghouse the night Collins was shot. Seven others testified that he was in the boardinghouse with them when someone arrived to spread the news about Collins, which is why they remembered that particular night.

The jury of farmers and ranchers was most interested in the buckshot pattern that Bulkeley Wells had preserved in the window as he investigated the shooting. Steve Adams's confession described him standing about seventy feet away, uphill from the building. The jury studied the pattern and unanimously determined that it could only have been created from about twenty feet away and not from uphill. Steve Adams was acquitted.

The verdict was a vindication for the union, since the scenario presented by the prosecution was that Adams had been hired by the union to kill Collins.

The murder of Arthur Collins was never solved.

THE SNOWY ADVENTURES OF THE MILLIONAIRE KID

B ecause of his taste for the finer things in life, the young man had earned the nickname around Telluride's saloons as the "Millionaire Kid." Others called him a "rooster."

The twenty-one year old "Kid's" adventures began on a snowy February day in 1911 when he cashed a Smuggler-Union check for $64.10 at the Corner Beer Hall. The check was made out to a fellow named Willard Hyatt, whose signature was already written on the back. When the Kid presented it, he signed the name "Earl Howard" beneath Hyatt's signature. The proprietor, Mr. Schuler, cashed the check but later took another look. He belatedly observed that both signatures were in the same handwriting.

He contacted the law, and they quickly determined that the Kid worked for Willard Hyatt at the Smuggler-Union. Hyatt had broken his leg and was holed up in his cabin, being cared for by Mrs. Hyatt. The Hyatts had given the helpful Kid the combination to their mailbox so he could fetch the mail. Instead of delivering it, he opened Hyatt's letter from the company and extracted his Smuggler-Union paycheck.

Meanwhile, the Kid caught wind that the marshal wanted to talk to him about mail robbery and forgery. After first visiting his landlady, Mrs. Tallman, and gallantly paying her the rent he owed, he vanished.

In an isolated spot like Telluride, there weren't too many places one could disappear to—especially in February—so Undersheriff Walt Kenley and Marshal George Hall ambled over to the train station to watch for the fugitive. The Kid did not appear. Later, trainmen reported they had seen the Kid walking along the tracks. An investigation revealed footprints heading through the snow into the mountains between Telluride and Ophir. Not the brightest idea in mid-February.

Kenley formed a posse, and they followed the Kid's tracks up to the top of the mountain. There, the trail led into an area of woods inaccessible to the horses, so the posse returned to Telluride.

Kenley soon received a call from a rancher near Ophir who reported that the Kid had stopped by for breakfast. Kenley hitched a sleigh to a fresh team and took off, hoping to make it to Ophir before the Kid got there. That night, when the Kid staggered out of the snow-bound mountains, reaching Ophir at eleven o'clock, Kenley was there to greet him.

At first, the Kid denied knowing anything about anything, saying his name was Jones and that he'd come from somewhere to the south. Kenley gave him the opportunity to produce at least one person in Ophir who knew him as "Jones," which did not occur.

Finally, having walked over the mountains through three to six feet of snow in the dead of winter for nearly twenty miles—much of it in the dark—the Millionaire Kid was arrested and taken back to Telluride. The Kid, whose real name was James Hilton, confessed. Once installed in the town jail, he became "an inmate of the bastille and a second class boarder at the New Sheridan."[43] The New Sheridan, famous in the region for its fine dining, had a deal with law enforcement to provide its leftovers to the prisoners in the county jail.

On February 16, the Kid had his preliminary hearing. Sadly, he was unable to walk because his feet had frozen during his sojourn over the mountains. He was in a lot of pain and quite cranky. He entered a plea of guilty, refused to accept an attorney and would not tell the court a thing about himself or his family. When asked whether he could provide a $1,000 bond, he remained mum and was remanded to the county jail. A doctor was also sent along to look at his feet.

As it turned out, this was not the first forgery adventure for the Kid. A month earlier, he had cashed another check made out to his favorite victim, Willard Hyatt (or Willett Wyett or Hayatt).

Mail robbery is a federal crime, so U.S. authorities were soon chomping at the bit to get hold of the Millionaire Kid. San Miguel County, however, held tight for the time being, feeling that it had a better shot with forgery charges.

The Kid was in the news again a couple weeks later. He was miffed because the New Sheridan's greedy guests were eating all the ice cream and there was none left over for him. The lad was so annoyed at this deprivation that he "grew obstreperous. He declared himself on a strike, screamed and cursed, and generally made the place unpleasant for the prisoners and undersheriff Kenley. The strike, in the end, proved fruitless and icecreamless."[44]

On the evening of April 21, the Kid proved he was more than just a pretty face when he used a case knife to remove three small screws from the bolt on his cell door and escape. His cellmates, Tony Sardini (the fellow who had threatened Jesse Munn) and J.T. Thompson, both facing charges of attempted murder, chose to stay put.

Undersheriff Kenley discovered him missing about ten minutes later during his 9:00 p.m. check. He and Sheriff Tallman mounted up and tracked the Kid all night long. Apparently, Hilton had not learned any lessons from his previous trek and had headed once more into the heavy spring snows of the San Juans. This time he made it all the way down the canyon and up onto Hastings Mesa, north of Sawpit. There, he walked easily on top of a crust of snow that caused much grief for the horse-mounted men following him.

Once again, the Kid's appetite got the better of him, and he stopped at the ranch of Charles Byfield. Unbeknownst to the hungry fugitive, Mr. Byfield had already been notified to be on the lookout for him. While Mrs. Byfield fed the Kid breakfast, Mr. Byfield excused himself and telephoned authorities. He later reported that the Kid took off in the direction of the Dallas Divide.

Marshal Hall rode the train to the Dallas Divide and scouted around. He soon discovered the well-fed Kid having himself a little nap along the train tracks and took him back to jail.

Finally, in May, James Hilton appeared before Judge Sprigg Shackleford, who gave him a sentence of one to fourteen years at the reformatory in Buena Vista. The judge also delivered a sober lecture about how his behavior would determine whether he would be locked up for one year or closer to fourteen years.

James Hilton apparently pleased his jailers at Buena Vista, as the news broke only six months later that he had been released and was spotted in Ouray. Irate comments appeared in the local papers, asking, "What's the Use?"

It appears that the Millionaire Kid may have learned his lesson, though, as no further corrections records exist for the hungry mountaineering lad—at least not in Colorado.

After this episode, there was much serious discussion in Telluride about building a proper jail.

WHERE IS JAMES O'KELLY?

So read the headline in the *San Miguel Examiner* on August 21, 1909.

A week earlier, the jovial, brogue-speaking, 210-pound Irishman, beloved by family, friends and customers, had vanished from the streets of Telluride. Those tracing "Jolly Jim's" movements that summer night learned that the Telluride saloonkeeper left his American House bar at about nine o'clock. Before taking off, O'Kelly opened his safe, pocketing a thick wad of bills and a six-shooter. He then made an unusual request. He asked a friend sitting at the bar to come by in the morning and watch the place for a few hours. The friend told him he had to head up the hills on Sunday afternoon to start work Monday morning, and O'Kelly assured him he'd be back in plenty of time. Then he left the saloon.

About ten o'clock, Mrs. O'Kelly phoned the saloon looking for her husband   . She was told he'd left an hour earlier. Her worry increased during the night when he did not return home, and by the next morning, she was anxious enough to institute a search for him around Telluride. They found no trace of him, but on Sunday night, folks arriving in town said they'd seen him near Sawpit, trudging along through rain and mud. He had exchanged greetings with them, and they thought nothing of the encounter until they reached Telluride and learned that he was missing.

Perhaps it wasn't completely out of the question that O'Kelly might just take off. Seven years earlier, in 1902, he had hopped on the train one morning with nowhere in particular to go, announcing that he "might" be back that evening. That time he came back.

What puzzled folks was that forty-two-year-old James O'Kelly adored his wife and three children. Katherine O'Kelly couldn't have been a more devoted wife. His beloved daughter Nellie, fourteen years old, frequently appeared in the papers for her piano recitals. There were also thirteen-year-old Kathleen and their ten-year-old son, Francis. James O'Kelly had been devastated five years earlier, in March 1904, when he and Katherine made the pilgrimage up to Lone Tree Cemetery to bury their fourth child, a baby girl. It wasn't like him to hurt those he loved.

Still, he'd been gone for a week, and some said he'd been acting awfully strangely in the days before he disappeared.

It was true that O'Kelly was a restless man. In October 1905, he bought out his partner in the American House, and only five months later he announced he was selling the place and moving to Silverton, where he had purchased the Branch Saloon. When heavy springs snows prevented him from leaving in March as he had planned, he grew anxious and restless. He left town as soon as the snows permitted. On May 31, 1906, his family followed suit and joined the "happy-go-lucky" Jimmy in their new Silverton home. He renamed his new saloon "Kelly's Place" and went to work making a success of it.

Their new life in Silverton lasted only a couple years. In the spring of 1908, Jolly Jim announced that "he had grown tired fighting ghosts on the banks of Cement creek and that he much preferred the companionship of the 'Good People' of Carlow [Ireland]."[45] He turned Kelly's Place over to his brother John and left.

The O'Kellys did not move to Ireland but instead returned to Telluride. There, he once again assumed control of the American House while his family settled back into the life they'd left behind two years earlier. Fifteen months later, he vanished.

On Monday, August 23, 1909, the mystery deepened as word reached Telluride that O'Kelly had been seen getting off the train in Placerville. There, he stopped and drank some coffee at Fred Surprise's hotel and then went to George King's place and chatted for a time. At some point, he suddenly vanished from the building.

At sundown that day, he turned up at a ranch on Hastings Mesa to visit his friend, Charles Byfield (the same Byfields who fed the Millionaire Kid). There, he had supper and went to bed but rose again at midnight. Despite the protests of his hosts, he left the house during a driving rain, saying he must get to Sawpit.

The next day, Tuesday, the "runaway husband" story became more complicated. O'Kelly appeared at the Gallagher ranch on the Dallas Divide. Mr. Gallagher, an old friend of the O'Kellys, recognized that something was amiss with his pal and managed to coax the .45-caliber six-shooter away from him. Shortly after, O'Kelly threw a fit and turned violent, making his host very grateful he'd got the gun away from him in time. O'Kelly finally calmed down, and when his friends weren't looking, he disappeared once again.

A story emerged much later that while Jim was there, Mr. Gallagher offered him an unidentified "stimulant," but O'Kelly refused, saying he had "cut it out" two years before.[46]

On Tuesday night, O'Kelly took shelter at the section house on Dallas hill, about halfway down the divide. (A section house was a large building that housed railroad men and their families who managed a particular section of railroad track.) O'Kelly spent several hours in the place, during which he threw another violent fit that shocked everyone. Once again, he disappeared without explanation. That was the last anyone saw of Jolly Jim O'Kelly.

After getting these tips, Mrs. O'Kelly and her brother, Alderman T.B. McMahon, arrived in Ridgeway and organized search parties. Joined by friends and relatives, including Jim's brother John, they scoured the rugged countryside around Ridgeway and north to Montrose. Days later, they had found no sign of the missing man. Folks were giving up hope that they would find him alive.

An investigation revealed no financial or other troubles that might have caused this sudden aberrant behavior, nor could anyone explain the violent fits described by those who had seen him. He had apparently taken $2,000 or $3,000 from his safe, so it was conceivable that he had simply abandoned his life and gone off to "fight ghosts" on his own.

Katherine O'Kelly and the children simply had to wait for word. In early November, when Jolly Jim had been missing more than two months, the family offered a $100 reward for information about their beloved father and husband.

The following spring, in May 1910, they still had no word. At that time, a resident of Dallas Divide, a man named Sim Noel, called Sheriff McKnight, saying he had information about O'Kelly. He told the sheriff he needed to make a warrant to search the premises of the section house where O'Kelly had last been seen. It was located at a place called Hillside, near a ranch belonging to a Mr. Von Hagen, on the Southern rail line. Noel referred to it as the "Italian section house."

Noel made a compelling enough case, and the sheriff, along with Mrs. O'Kelly, her attorney and Sim Noel, searched the section house and questioned its residents. They came away with nothing except a conviction that the folks there knew nothing about what happened to O'Kelly. They said O'Kelly had quickly downed four glasses of water that night but ate nothing. He left in the morning, walking unsteadily down the railroad tracks.

It wasn't clear what Sim Noel had told the sheriff before they embarked upon this latest search, but the story soon emerged that Noel's daughter, Mrs. Louis Fournier, had encountered a psychic medium in Kansas City who told her that O'Kelly had been beaten over the head with a club and killed, and that he was buried near the section house. The medium had told Mrs. Fournier that O'Kelly had from $2,500 to $3,000 on his person when he disappeared and that the motive for the murder was robbery. Mrs. Fournier had told Mrs. O'Kelly about it, and Mrs. O'Kelly had sworn out the original search warrant, which was served to the sheriff by Sim Noel.

Another year and a half went by without news of Jolly Jim. Katherine never gave up searching for her husband, traveling frequently to the Ridgeway area, posting rewards and organizing search parties.

On Friday, October 20, 1911, Katherine learned that someone had found a coat near an abandoned railroad bridge on the Dallas Divide. Accompanied by Father Brunner, she traveled to the site, a place called Pleasant Valley. There they were met by a large party of men and women on horseback, who showed them the discovered items.

Katherine identified the coat as the one her husband was wearing when he disappeared. The group began searching the immediate area. About two hundred yards away from the spot where the coat was found, one of the searchers stumbled upon the remains of a man. Despite the advanced stage of decomposition, Katherine managed to make a formal identification of her husband based on the clothing and contents of his pockets.

More than two years after Jolly Jim vanished, his body made its final journey back to Telluride. The coroner could find no indication that he had died of anything other than natural causes, though there was still no explanation for his mysterious behavior. On his body, they found a watch and chain, keys, a bank book and a prayer book. One odd detail was that the watch was not O'Kelly's expensive gold watch but a cheap silver one that the family did not recognize. This led to speculation that a thief had swapped watches with him.

They also discovered a wad of tattered and faded paper, which they at first guessed was the $2,000 or $3,000 in bills he was said to have with him. (Another report said he carried gold coins.) However, the wad turned out to be two small notebooks that had formed into a clump. The only money they found on him was two five-cent pieces. This gave rise to two theories—that he was murdered and robbed or that someone had looted the body after he died.

Searchers who had been involved from the beginning insisted they had scoured the area before and suggested that someone had recently dumped the body there. It was found in plain view of an abandoned bridge over a small creek. An old campfire was spotted nearby.

In describing the discovery, the *San Miguel Examiner* wrote much about O'Kelly's devoted wife, Katherine:

> *She never rested a moment from the time of his disappearance until the bones were identified, and even now at times she almost feels as if he will come to her again in life. She kept up a continued search for his remains, made trip after trip to Dallas Divide, went to Denver once where it was thought his body had been found, and went to other places seeking always some clue that would lead her to him, and the strain has told on her...*

Several members of the O'Kelly family, including "Jolly Jim," are buried at Telluride's historic Lone Tree Cemetery. *Photo by the author.*

Through Examiner, Mrs. O'Kelly wishes to thank all those who were kind to her, aided in her search, sympathized with her, and especially does she feel thankful to Mr. and Mrs. Louis Fournier, who did so much at so many times while she was searching for the remains on Dallas Divide, near their home. They met her, gave her assistance, and cared for her just like she was one of the family.[47]

On Monday, October 23, 1911, family and friends held a service for James O'Kelly at St. Patrick's Church, with Reverend Father Brunner presiding. O'Kelly's casket was swathed in flowers. Those grieving had endured a long two years of uncertainty since his disappearance and were still saddled with the mysterious circumstances of his death. After the service, a long procession marched to the Lone Tree Cemetery, where James O'Kelly was laid to rest next to the grave of his little girl who had died as an infant.

In the years after James O'Kelly's death, Katherine O'Kelly ran a rooming house in Telluride. She died in 1920, nine years after she found her husband. Nellie (Mary Ellen) O'Kelly married George Mathison in 1918. The couple lived in Pandora, where they had a son named Francis; they later moved to Quincy, Massachusetts. Daughter Kathleen became a teacher in Telluride and later in Salt Lake City. Son Francis went to engineering school at the University of Colorado at Boulder.

SAN MIGUEL COUNTY
BANK ROBBERY

On June 24, 1889, three men rode into Telluride, all gussied up in "silver-studded bridles, spurs, saddles, and artillery, five-gallon hats, red bandannas, flash shirts, chaps, and high-heel cowboy boots."[48] Some may have recognized them as they ambled down Main Street—they'd recently been in town winning plenty of money on a horse named Betty. They were Matt Warner; Warner's brother-in-law, Tom McCarty; and LeRoy "Butch" Parker, later known as Butch Cassidy.

The well-dressed trio stopped their horses in front of the San Miguel County Bank. Matt and Butch dismounted and strolled into the bank while Tom waited with the horses. No one was inside but the cashier—some reports say the man was Charles Painter, future owner of the *Telluride Journal*. Butch and Matt smiled at the fellow, quickly checked the place out and then

> [m]y gun is under his nose before he has time to see me draw it. Butch barges right into the cage where the cashier is like he owns it. The cashier don't have to be invited to stick up his hands. They are already up. He looks scared and sick and licked.
>
> "Put all the money in that sack," says I to Butch, "and pass it through the window."
>
> Butch puts enough money in the sack to choke a cow and hands it to me. I notice the vault is open.
>
> "Get into the vault," I tell Butch, "and get the big money."
>
> He comes out in a minute with a sack loaded with bales of greenbacks and a lotta gold.[49]

LeRoy Parker, also known as Butch Cassidy, started his criminal career by robbing the San Miguel County Bank in Telluride. *Library of Congress, Prints & Photographs Division.*

The robbers pushed the cashier out into the street at gunpoint and then released him, jumped on their horses and stampeded gloriously out of town, while "[t]he crowd just look[ed] on paralyzed, helpless, and dumb."[50]

The robbers galloped into the open country toward the Mancos Mountains, laughing and hooting it up over how easy it had been. Until trouble arrived. "Then something happened that couldn't happen more than once in a thousand years. We had to cross a road. Right where we had to cross two fellers was riding, and one of 'em knew us."[51] The robbers tried to hide their faces, but it was too late. They'd been recognized.

Some accounts say that the robbers holed up in the Ophir area, but Warner's autobiography says they rode south to the Mancos Mountains. There they began a lengthy game of cat and mouse with their pursuers. Knowing the law was now after him, Matt Warner gave away his ranch and horse herd—a loss of about $20,000 that far outweighed what he gained from the robbery. Stories vary on how much the haul was. Warner claims they took in $10,000 each, but other accounts vary from $10,000 to $20,000 in total.

In his autobiography, Matt Warner later wrote about the robbery:

> *The adventure seemed so great it purty near took our breaths away. We was range-riding cowboys that had operated entirely outside of the cities. Now we was going into another kind of world and a new kind of adventure. One of the big things that drew us into this new adventure was the chance it offered us to satisfy the old cowboy grudge against city smart alecks. We would ride right into town and show 'em who was smartest.*[52]

After a couple stints in prison, Matt Warner "went straight" in 1900 and made a home in Utah, where he held several positions in law enforcement over the next four decades. Butch Cassidy became a famous outlaw with his partner, the Sundance Kid, and, according to legend, died in a shower of bullets in Bolivia in 1908. In 1893, Tom McCarty, his brother Bill and Bill's son Fred robbed a Delta Bank and killed a teller. Reports varied as to which bandit shot the man. As the robbers galloped out of town, a sharpshooter named W. Ray Simpson who worked in the hardware store across the street shot Bill and Fred. Both died. Tom McCarty escaped. His eventual fate is a mystery, but some say he was shot to death in Montana around the turn of the century. Like Butch Cassidy, rumors abound that McCarty retired from the criminal life and lived quietly to an old age.

The money the three men stole from the San Miguel County Bank was never recovered.

THE LIFE AND TIMES OF
THE TREMONT SALOON

O f the many dozens of saloons that lubricated the difficult lives of Telluride's early citizens, one of the most prominent was the Tremont. Opened sometime during the 1880s by a man named George Miller, the Tremont was located next door to the San Miguel County Bank. The saloon went through several owners during its colorful thirty-year life as a hub of Telluride society. In the late 1890s, it was owned by a partnership of two men—a thirty-five-year-old Ohio man, Joseph Piquard, and a German immigrant named "Colonel" Fred Kuster. They spruced up the place by painting it white and installing a handsome pair of plate-glass windows in front. They also added an Orchestral Regina, an elegant coin-operated jukebox made of mahogany that played music recorded on giant steel discs.

In the wee hours of an October morning in 1897, the saloon was still hopping with the late-night crowd—some gambling, others huddled around the warm stove. Suddenly, a fellow at the stove gave a signal, and he and two others rose and produced "long, blue-barreled 45-calibre Colts revolvers in their hands."[53] They ordered everyone to put up their hands and then lined them up in front of the bar. In the next room, several Swedes had been enjoying a boisterous card game. As a robber herded them into the main room, one man escaped.

The house had apparently been losing that evening, and the robbers collected only about $100 from the faro table. They failed to pry open the cash register, which was secured with a combination lock. The unfortunate bartender, Fred Horton, was relieved of a $150 diamond stud and his watch chain.

A street in 1896 Telluride. *U.S. Geological Survey Photographic Library.*

The robbers were impatient, as they were aware of the escaped Swedish card player. (As it turned out, the Swede ran off instead of going for help.) They soon vanished out the back door, having missed the $600 bank roll from the evening's activity at the roulette table and $500 to $600 in cash that was in an unlocked drawer they failed to check, plus an equal amount of cash in the safe, which was also unlocked.

All three robbers were soon identified. One was "the son of Bob McCarthy [Tom McCarty], one of the men who robbed the San Miguel Valley [County] bank of this place a number of years ago."[54] Until recently, all three had worked at the Tomboy Mine.

The next morning, three local men reported that their horses had been stolen overnight, and authorities guessed the culprits had been the Tremont robbers. A posse tracked the men up to the Dallas Divide, where they lost the trail amid too many other tracks. They questioned locals, who reported seeing two of the robbers with fresh mounts, driving their fatigued horses in front of them. The posse picked up the trail again near the tiny settlement of Dallas (located north of Ridgeway at today's intersection of Highway

550 and Colorado Road 24). From there, the tracks led toward Gunnison. Unfortunately, the posse's horses were exhausted by then, and they figured the robbers had a forty- to fifty-mile head start. They gave up the chase, and the robbers were never caught.

In the spring of 1899, the five-foot, five-inch, round-faced Piquard bought out his partner and, for the next thirteen years, went back and forth between leasing out the Tremont and running the place himself. During that period, his wife, Maggie, died and he went abroad for a year.

The Tremont was robbed again on an August evening in 1901. On this occasion, two men wearing bandannas over their faces burst in the back door and lined everyone up at gunpoint. Between the faro table and cash register, they got about $250. While the robbery was in progress, a local doctor, Dr. deLanney, started to enter the saloon and saw what was going on. He quickly sounded the alarm, but by the time the marshal arrived, the robbers had already snuck out the back door and down the dark alley, making off on their horses. Their pursuers nearly caught up with them, but the robbers fired off several shots, hitting Night Marshal Corey in the calf with buckshot. Corey shot back and thought he hit one of them, but these robbers were never caught either.

The Tremont Saloon offered far more than just a place to have a drink or hand over your money to a robber. It was an important social center where you could play faro or roulette in the game rooms, place bets on elections and boxing matches and partake of raffles and pool tournaments. On election day, the Tremont served as a polling station. Joe Piquard even produced art calendars for sale.

Piquard, who was also part owner of the famed Cosmopolitan Saloon, intended to make the Tremont one of the handsomest in the region—installing new wallpaper, fresh paint and stylish wainscoting. In 1901, a new manager, S.H. Matthews, continued with the policy of keeping the Tremont as a "first class resort."[55] In 1906, the Tremont was one of the first Telluride establishments to install a gas lighting system. The saloon also installed its own firefighting equipment and was one of the first places in town to put in a concrete sidewalk in front.

Despite its upscale reputation, the Tremont was the scene of at least two violent deaths. On a pleasant August afternoon in 1904, gunfire erupted between two men inside the saloon. The quarrel had started months earlier in another saloon when Fred Leaming accused the bartender there of short-changing him. Lola "Lo" Umstead, the bartender in question, took issue with the accusation. Both men were well known in the region. On the morning of the shooting, twenty-seven-year-old Umstead armed himself and told others he was going to settle the thing.

When Umstead found Leaming at the Tremont, he tried to hit him with the gun. Leaming dodged the blow, pulled his gun and got off five shots, four of those going point blank into Umstead. The Tremont bartender, Frank Maisey, tried to intervene and took a bullet in his arm.

When the doctor arrived, Umstead was on the floor in critical condition. His last words were a request to be buried beside his mother at the Lone Tree Cemetery. Leaming was arrested but later acquitted by the coroner's jury, who ruled the shooting "justifiable and not felonious."[56]

Another tragic shooting death occurred in the saloon in March 1906. Abiel (or Albert) Tervo and his brother Victor, two Finnish immigrants, were reportedly drunk already when they entered the Tremont on that early spring night. Victor ordered a series of drinks at the bar and then headed into the gambling room without paying. The story on the streets was that "forgetting" to pay was habitual behavior for him. He had also aroused some curiosity after he was caught stealing clothes from a local sporting woman.

On this occasion, the bartender followed Victor to the faro table, insisting on payment. A scuffle followed, and Abiel jumped in to help his brother. The man running the nearby roulette table, Hermann Dahlberg, intervened, punching Abiel in the head. Abiel staggered back and fell to the floor. When the brawl ended, several men hoisted Abiel into a chair and realized that he seemed to be near death. They called Dr. Murray Hadley, who reported that Abiel's neck was broken. He died within half an hour.

Hermann Dahlberg was arrested. At his trial a couple months later, his defense was that he was just trying to help the bartender and that he hadn't meant to kill Tervo. After a ten-minute discussion, the jury ruled him "not guilty."

In 1908 and 1909, as part of a regional crackdown and a morality campaign on the part of certain politicians, city officials arrested a number of Telluride's saloonkeepers, claiming with great consternation that illegal gambling was going on in the town. The Tremont was first to go before the judge.

A fellow named George A. Nicol indignantly testified that he had witnessed "the mechanism and operation of the roulette wheel and faro game, and declared he knew what he was talking about."[57] The defense pointed out that Mr. Nicol had recently run for mayor on the Municipal Reform ticket, which was anti–dance halls, anti-gambling and anti-alcohol. They claimed he was seeking revenge because he lost.

The Tremont case resulted in a hung jury. Eventually, the parties cut a deal, and the crowd of defendants pleaded guilty and paid a fine of thirty dollars each.

In 1912, Joseph Piquard's on-again, off-again relationship with the Tremont appeared to end when he sold the building to Morris Lehmann of the National Club. Two popular Telluride businessmen, Charles Kearney and "Fatty" Burgwin, took over proprietorship of the saloon. Kearney and Burgwin created a splash in town when they presented their Christmas customers that year with an ice sculpture of a four-foot-high bowl filled with delicious punch. They adorned the ice bowl with "a tiny Christmas tree bearing presents for several hundred persons."[58] They also lured customers with wired-in results of elections, boxing matches and football and baseball games; a turkey raffle; roast turkey lunches; and, best of all, free hot roast beef "lunches" every Saturday night. In 1913, they installed a pay telephone (invented in 1889). When World War I started in the summer of 1914, the Tremont kept its patrons updated with war bulletins each day from 11:00 a.m. to 4:00 p.m.

The saloon and its patrons were shocked one day when the big-hearted "Fatty" Burgwin, while sitting at a table in the Tremont, abruptly slumped in his chair. Burgwin, who had grown up in Rico, Colorado, was pronounced dead of a heart attack on October 8, 1913. His partner, Kearney, continued on as sole proprietor.

One popular "mixologist" at the Tremont was an amiable young fellow named Pete Wakeline. The Tremont ran numerous ads extolling Pete's signature drink, called a "Tremont Flip."[59] Pete also gained popularity in town for concocting a green St. Patrick's Day punch. His doings were regularly reported in the local papers as he took fishing trips to Lake City and attended the races in Durango.

On the morning of December 31, 1914, the Tremont was the scene of yet another early morning robbery. This daring episode was a bit different than previous robberies. At about three o'clock in the morning, two armed men entered through the front door. One of the fellows had a bandanna over the lower part of his face and two strips of court plaster (an early type of bandage) covering portions of his upper face. The other covered his face with a white handkerchief. Both carrying .45-caliber weapons, they forced the saloon's dozen or so occupants into a line with their hands up. One bandit stood guard over them while the other gathered bank rolls from the various games into an ore sack. The bandits then forced the victims into a boiler room at the rear of the saloon and went to work on the cash register at the front.

One man being held hostage, William Driscoll, managed to slip through a window in the bathroom and notify Night Marshal Clarence Tyler. Tyler snuck into the saloon and aimed his weapon at the robber who was crouched in front of the safe. Before Tyler could take any further action, the other robber shot him from behind. Tyler fired off a couple of wild shots, and the robber working on the safe fired back at him. Both robbers ran out the front door and escaped up the street. William Driscoll saw their escape and got off a few shots, following their trail as far as the cemetery. Other citizens heard the commotion and fired at the robbers as well.

Tyler managed to walk over to Dr. Hadley's office. Aside from an injury over the night marshal's eye from flying glass, the doctor also found a bullet wound in his ear. All agreed that Tyler's survival was miraculous, and the townsfolk hailed him as a hero for his courage.

Theories instantly circulated about the robbery, which resulted in the loss of about $600. Many remarked on the apparent careful planning. The robbers knew the saloon's layout, understood how it operated and knew that it would be open later than usual that night. The sheriff's office soon took several men into custody. The suspects were two men named Bob White and Frank Marrs and—to the town's shock and dismay—the Tremont's popular bartender, celebrated for the "Tremont Flip," Pete Wakeline. After a couple days' discussion at the jail, on January 5, Frank Marrs and Pete Wakeline confessed.

In May 1915, sharing local headlines with the sinking of the ocean liner *Lusitania*, Frank Marrs and Pete Wakeline went on trial. Frank Marrs was a forty-six-year-old paroled convict and a gambler. He had served seven of a twelve- to fourteen-year sentence on a charge of assault with attempt to murder, having been paroled from the Colorado State Penitentiary in April 1909. Twenty-six-year-old Pete Wakeline was born and raised in Colorado and had no prior record.

After a plea bargain, Wakeline was charged with larceny and given a nine- to ten-year sentence in the penitentiary. Marrs was charged with robbery and given the same sentence. Although both men had fired at Marshal Tyler and Marrs had put a steel-capped bullet in the lawman's head from a .32-20 pistol, neither was charged with attempted murder.

Wakeline's attorney, angered at what he deemed a harsh sentence, threatened to take the case to a higher court and asked for a new trial. He said the sentence had not been clarified when Wakeline agreed to the plea. Wakeline soon gave up the fight, however, and was taken off to Cañon City to begin serving his sentence. After serving three years, he was paroled in September 1917. Marrs got out on parole in June 1919.

No.9567 Peter Wakeline
Received May 20 1915
County San Miguel
Crime Larceny
Sentence 9 to 10 years
Occupation Bar Tender

Age 26: Weight 144:Height 5-8 1/2: Complexion
sallow: Bust 37:Waist 36:Thigh 20:Neck 15:
Hat 7: Shoes 7 1/2:Hair Brown:Eyes Gray:
Build Slender: Nat American.

Scar on fore head:Scar on lower lip: Teeth fair
2 upper left & 1 lower right gone:

Above: Mug shot of Pete Wakeline, famous for the "Tremont Flip." *Colorado State Archives.*

Left: Wakeline's Record of Convict. *Colorado State Archives.*

Meanwhile, in anticipation of the new Colorado state law against the sale of alcohol, Charles Kearney sadly announced the closure of the Tremont in December 1915 with a brief poem in the paper: "Good-bye little bar, good-bye. You'll be a drugstore, bye and bye."[60] On January 1, 1916, the state of Colorado officially went dry.

THE DISAPPEARANCE OF
A TOMBOY BRIDE

On a bright Thursday morning in August 1911, Mrs. Anna Borg left her small home at the Tomboy Mine, planning to walk down the long, rugged road into Telluride, where she would shop, pay bills for her husband and visit friends.

She never showed up.

Born in Finland, twenty-six-year-old Anna was a tiny woman—five feet tall, with a slight build and dark complexion. She had only been married two years when she vanished from the Tomboy road. Her husband, Lee Borg, worked as a miner at the Tomboy.

Within a day or two, an ugly rumor surfaced that Anna had eloped with a fellow Finn named Isaac Matson. Matson had apparently known Anna back in Finland and was said to be smitten with her. He had also disappeared. Her husband vehemently denied this rumor, saying that he and Anna enjoyed a happy home life. Lee Borg offered a reward for information about his wife's whereabouts, saying she had been carrying about $150, along with a gold watch and several gold rings, one of them engraved with the names of the husband and wife.

Once the reward was offered, search parties began to scour the many cliffs and ravines between the Tomboy Mine up in Savage Basin and the town of Telluride, nearly three thousand feet below. Someone claimed they had spotted her that day at the Alleghany Mine above Telluride, which narrowed the search area considerably, but searchers still could find no trace of Anna Borg.

On Saturday morning, a group of young boys came forward and declared that they had seen Anna board an outbound train at the Telluride depot.

Because of this news, the search stopped. By Monday morning, officials had determined that the boys had lied and resumed searching.

Nearly a week after her disappearance, on Wednesday, August 23, 1911, a searcher named Robert Ebb was checking a ravine above Pandora when he heard the distinctive sound of many flies buzzing. He climbed up into the ravine and saw what looked like rags. As he continued on, he spotted a pair of feet.

He lingered only long enough to determine that it was a woman's body and then hurried back to town. Sheriff Tallman, Coroner Taylor and several others drove up to Pandora and then followed Ebb on foot to the spot in the ravine. There they found Anna Borg about five hundred feet above the Smuggler Mill. They carried her body down to the wagon at Pandora, drove her into town and then had the unhappy chore of notifying her husband.

Anna's pocketbook and gold watch were missing from her person, but searchers eventually discovered both in the cliffs above where she was found. The pocketbook still contained the $150, and the watch was smashed. These clues pointed at a motive other than robbery.

The area above the gulch showed signs that she may have been carried off the road and tossed over the cliff, which was about 150 feet from the road. She fell at least 700 feet. A ledge jutted out about 100 feet wide above where

A view of Savage Basin, where the Tomboy Mine is located. The road down to Telluride can be seen on the far mountainside. *U.S. Geological Survey Photographic Library.*

Anna Borg disappeared while walking along this road that leads three thousand feet down from the Tomboy Mine to Telluride. *Library of Congress, Prints & Photographs Division.*

her body was found, and they concluded that it would have caught her body had she simply slipped and fallen.

Further indication of foul play lay in the fact that the buttons of her clothing had been ripped open "in a manner that could not have resulted from the fall."[61]

Talk of lynching circulated throughout Telluride as the coroner went to work on the body, trying to determine whether she'd been dead or alive when she went over the cliff. Attention focused on Isaac Matson, a former Tomboy employee. The day after Anna's disappearance, Matson abruptly withdrew $4,000 from his bank in Telluride and bought a ticket for Brooklyn, New

York, saying he was going back home to Finland. His co-workers claimed he had said nothing prior to that about leaving. Unsubstantiated stories surfaced about Matson following Anna when she left the Tomboy at about 7:30 on the morning of her death. He had been seen around 11:00 a.m. when he called at the Tomboy offices to collect his wages.

A man named Charles Malloy came forward, saying he had seen Anna near the cliff but did not see Matson. Some suggested she may have committed suicide, but others argued that the spot where she went over was difficult to get to and there were other, more accessible places. They also pointed out that she had no motive to do herself in, that she'd only been married less than two years and had a good home life.

When the coroner's report came out, it did not say for certain what killed her. The official verdict was death resulting from a fall over the cliff with "attendant circumstances unknown."[62] Testimony about the condition of the body was gruesome, describing how the head was crushed and nearly severed and how, when they lifted her into the basket, one of her arms nearly came off.

Once the allegations against Isaac Matson began to emerge, friends of his spoke up. They insisted that he was incapable of such an act and that he would return to Telluride to clear his name, suggesting that he didn't tell anyone about his trip because he wanted to surprise his friends in Finland. Isaac Matson never returned to Telluride, and the mystery of Anna Borg's death on the Tomboy road was never solved.

In June 1915, Lee Borg died alone in his cabin after a long battle with nephritis. Although he was only thirty-nine, the newspaper described him as an "aged resident of this city" who had "been a county charge for some time past and has no near relatives as far as is known."[63] Notices of his death mentioned that his wife had been killed in a fall over the cliffs. Both Lee and Anna Borg were buried at Lone Tree Cemetery.

BANQUETS AT THE
TELLURIDE TREASURY

Of the many public servants entrusted with guarding the public treasury, there are always a few who are "unfortunate in not being able to distinguish county money from [their] own."[64] One such distinguished fellow was Harry L. Servis. Editor of the *Telluride Journal* in the mid-1890s, Servis ran successfully for San Miguel county clerk and recorder on the People's Party ticket in 1897. Servis first took the oath of office on January 11, 1898, and was later reelected. He was also deputized on occasion, such as June 1897, when Sheriff Downtain asked Servis to help escort a convicted highgrader to the penitentiary. He was married to Nellie G. Servis, and the couple had a little boy named Frederick, born in 1896.

Though Servis was a highly respected citizen of Telluride with friends everywhere, his excellent career headed south in 1901. On September 7 of that year, Servis abruptly resigned as county clerk and was replaced by W. Robinson, the deputy clerk. Servis took a job at the Tomboy Mine for a few months and then moved to Denver in the spring of 1902. It was probably no coincidence that in April 1902, the county attorney filed charges against the former clerk, saying that Servis had used county funds for his own private use.

In early May, the Denver papers were abuzz with reports that Servis had been arrested there by an Arapahoe County sheriff on charges from Telluride. Authorities stated that he had "forged the names of persons to county warrants, had them cashed and misappropriated the money."[65] The charges shocked everyone in Telluride. Unconfirmed reports said the amount taken was between $500 and $1,000. Depending on the type of calculation used, this amounts to somewhere between $13,000 and $640,000 in today's

Harry Servis looks a bit surprised to find himself the subject of a mug shot. *Colorado State Archives.*

```
#5488            Harry L. Servis.
Rec'd            June 20, 02.
County           San Miguel.
Crime            Embezzlwment.
Term             1 to 3 yrs.
Age 37  Occu.    Printer.
Weight 126       Build Slender.
Height 5'6-1/2"  Eyes Gray.
Hair Dark        Comp. Dark.

        MARKS AND SCARS:
scar above right clavicle: scar
on left side of ferehead: small
scar under right jaw:vaccination
mark left arm.
```

Record of Convict for Harry Servis. *Colorado State Archives.*

dollars.[66] Mrs. Servis "encumbered" her house to pay the debt down to $200 or $300. Friends of the family donated to the cause, feeling sorry for Mrs. Servis. Since her husband had stepped down as county clerk, she had been obliged to take work as a book agent for a publishing house.

On May 8, 1902, Servis appeared before Justice Holmes and pleaded not guilty. He did not make bail. By May 31, Servis had changed his plea to guilty of embezzlement, and a few weeks later he was sentenced to one to three years.

On June 19, 1902, Harry Servis, who once escorted a prisoner, was himself escorted by Sheriff Rutan to Cañon City. After he settled in, he was such a model prisoner that they allowed him to wear civilian clothing and assigned him to serve on the "welcoming committee" for new prisoners.

Meanwhile, Mrs. Servis moved with her little boy to Creede, where she had a sister, Mrs. Webber, who unfortunately died unexpectedly in May 1903. Harry Servis was paroled that same month, after serving about a year, and his sentence was discharged on January 11, 1905. The Servis family later moved to Denver and eventually to Golden, where Harry worked in the newspaper business as a printer.

A few years later, the haul of public funds pocketed by Harry Servis would look like peanuts. In April 1900, Peter A. Lilley moved with his wife, Molly, from San Bernardo to Telluride. There he took up duties as the new county assessor. Later on, he became Telluride city clerk and secretary of the school board. He also served as treasurer for the Elks Club and the Telluride band.

Seven years after he first took office, on May 27, 1907, Peter A. Lilley was arrested and thrown in jail for embezzling public funds. The *Telluride Journal* introduced the story under a two-column headline:

In its experience of a quarter of a century, as chronicler and purveyor of news to the people of Telluride and San Miguel county, a more unpleasant duty has not befallen the Journal than that which confronts it today.

Peter A. Lilley, a respected citizen of this community for more than a score of years, during which time he has been an honored and trusted public official in various capacities, being at present city clerk and secretary director of the school board, was arrested about 6 o'clock last evening...

It is doubtful if Telluride has ever experienced a more severe shock than that which followed the announcement last evening of the crime and the arrest of Mr. Lilley. People were loth to believe it and demanded the fullest confirmation before accepting the rumor.[67]

According to one story, the embezzlement scheme was revealed when members of city council decided to examine the books, hoping to find ways to battle the town's growing deficit. Another version had the theft uncovered by Joseph Piquard at the Tremont Saloon. Piquard was suspicious about a check presented by Lilley for $321, made out to a water supply company. He took the check to city offices, where they discovered that it corresponded to an entry in the city's books for $3.

Either way, officials quickly began a thorough check of the town's books. "As warrant after warrant was found to have been raised in this manner, the sweat poured from the faces of the mayor and the one or two aldermen conducting the investigation."[68]

The city attorney filed a criminal complaint against Lilley. On the evening of May 27, Deputy Sheriff Knudtson walked into the Hub Saloon where Peter Lilley was playing cards and arrested him.

After first procuring Lilley's resignation, investigators soon determined how the embezzlement was committed, as described by the *Journal*:

> It appears that his method has been to draw warrants in the name of fictitious persons, for instance, a warrant in favor of John Doe for $3 in payment for a day's work on the street, forging the endorsement of the fictitious name, and presenting the same to the Mayor for his signature, which was of course readily affixed, then he would add one or two ciphers, making the warrant good for $30 or $300, and would procure the cash on it.[69]

This news created understandable anxiety for members of the Elks Club, school board and Telluride band, and all rushed to inspect their books. Folks at the Elks Club were horrified to find between $250 and $300 unaccounted for. The Telluride band discovered that its account had been relieved of every last penny. The school board treasurer was out of town, so officials were obliged to wait for his return before learning how bad it was.

It soon emerged what lay at the root of Peter Lilley's downfall—the money went "over the bar and the green cloth."[70] Three gambling spots in town—presumably where he had lost most of the public monies—quickly volunteered to help repay the stolen loot, hoping to fend off any public outrage against gambling.

Within a couple days, the amount embezzled by Lilley ballooned to more than $10,000. Depending on the method of calculation, $10,000 in 1907 would be worth somewhere between $236,000 and $4.3 million today.[71]

The school board treasurer returned and quickly discovered that at least $2,000 was missing from the school fund, most of the theft occurring in recent months. That investigation was far from finished. School officials feared that he had stolen as much from them as he had from the city. These thefts were particularly egregious, as many local citizens had invested their savings in school funds. For these folks, there was no insurance, and the losses came out of their pockets.

Friends and colleagues of Lilley who had initially tried to defend him began to drop off amid the growing chorus of outrage. It was clear that the only reason Lilley was able to get away with the outrageous thefts was because of his position of respect and trust in the community. Folks simply didn't question him—even though he must have been seen frequenting the town's gambling rooms.

The *Journal* reported that Mrs. Lilley was so shocked by the allegations that she collapsed. Unlike Mrs. Servis, she was unable to come up with any funds to cover her husband's misdeeds: "The residence is mortgaged for about $1,300 and there are a few other bills. There may be some mining property and the wife may have some resources but nothing like the amount of the shortage."[72]

The town of Telluride published a long list of warrants (checks) that it no longer intended to honor, as they had been discovered to be duplicates, modifications or outright forgeries created by Lilley. The victims squabbled at some length about who should get stuck holding the bag—the town, the bank or any of the numerous businesses that cashed bad checks.

Lilley himself displayed a fatalistic attitude, telling friends that he had expected to be caught for at least a year and was relieved that it was all over. He claimed he had meant to shoot himself when it all came out but his nerve failed him.

City Treasurer V.U. Rodgers and other officials spent long nights reviewing the books. They confirmed all the bad news, saying dryly that Lilley seemed to favor the number "6," getting the mayor to sign a check for $6 and later changing it to $60 or $600. Lilley had started his game back on March 7, 1896, giving him a career as an embezzler of more than ten years. In recent months, the number of checks Lilley wrote had increased dramatically. In the past month alone, he had written six phony checks.

Despite initial efforts of gambling establishments to "make up" for the losses, the Lilley scandal brought a temporary end to open gambling in Telluride. At 8:00 a.m. on Wednesday morning, May 29, 1907, "the Click of the Little Ivory Ball is no Longer Heard in Telluride," as the *Journal* announced on page one, next to several columns devoted to the Lilley story:[73]

The first gambling games in Telluride were opened with the starting of the camp in 1880, and they have continued uninterruptedly and unmolested ever since, with the exception of a brief period when the town was under martial law.

Telluride is the only town in the state that has not…encountered anti-gambling campaigns, due to a moral spasm or something of the kind…

The closing of the games is due to the Lilley scandal, it being claimed that the thousands of dollars he stole went into the drawers of the faro games. No sooner had his stealings became [sic] public then denunciation of gambling began and it is said that plans were formulating for legal procedure against the keepers of gambling houses. These men got together last evening and caucused on the situation, finally resolving to close all games this morning and pack away their paraphernalia.[74]

The ban on gambling soon expanded across the entire district under Judge Shackleford, which included eight counties.

As the investigation into Lilley's activities with the school fund continued, the amounts grew rapidly, along with the outrage of the people of Telluride. By May 31, the amount was $40,000. Under interrogation, Lilley revealed another method he used on the school fund. When a check was paid and marked as such on the back, he erased the "paid" stamp, somehow modified the date and amount and took the same check to the bank to cash it again.

Public sympathy for Mrs. Lilley increased drastically when it was revealed that she had also been a victim of her husband's thievery. She was an heiress to an estate back east, from which she received a periodic income. She turned these monies over to her husband, who supposedly purchased tax warrants as an investment. However, after showing her the documents, instead of putting them in the safe as promised, he cashed them and spent the money.

By late July, the investigations were complete. The school fund came out the biggest loser. Since the beginning of his work there in March 1902, Lilley had embezzled a little over $39,750 from Telluride schools. With his other thefts, Lilley's total haul was more than $46,000. In today's terms, commensurate amounts would range between $1,085,600 (based on the consumer price index) and $19,642,000 (based on relative share of GDP).[75]

In mid-November 1907, forty-nine-year-old Peter A. Lilley pleaded guilty to five indictments. Despite a plea for leniency from Congressman H.M. Hogg, Judge Sprigg Shackleford handed down a combined sentence of thirty-three to forty-two years (a variety of sentences ranging from six to ten years on each count), along with a lecture:

In some respects, the Court has felt that your wrong doing has been the result of weakness, but you are evidently a man of a good deal more than ordinary intelligence, a man who might have been a very useful citizen in this community; you were trusted by this community probably to a greater degree than any other man in it; you had charge of the public funds of the city and county, and furthermore of the most sacred of the public funds, the school funds of this district.

Your counsel has stated to me that you have been led into this wrong doing by the vice of gambling, which is the worst vice a man can indulge in. It leads to all other vices, and the history of gambling is written in blood; it is the mother of suicide and the mother of criminals.[76]

Anger and resentment apparently had short lives in the thin mountain air of frontier Telluride. When Peter A. Lilley had been in Cañon City for four years, a petition for a pardon began circulating. Promoted by Mrs. Lilley and the *Telluride Journal*, the petition was signed by hundreds of people, "showing the united sentiment in favor of the release of Mr. Lilley from prison."[77] Among the signatories were the entire grand jury who indicted Lilley. On Thursday, April 18, 1912, sharing the page with a banner headline describing

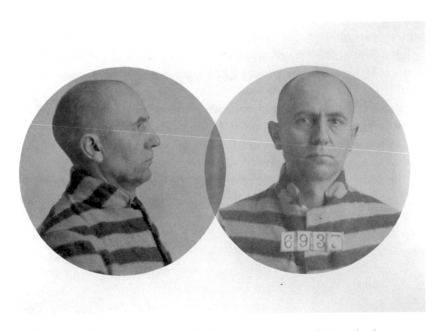

Peter Lilley embezzled every nickel he could find but was eventually forgiven by the town. *Colorado State Archives.*

```
  6937              Peter A. Lilley,
Recd               November 19/1907
County             San Miguel
Crime              Embezzlement (5 counts accumulative)
Term               33 to 42 years
Occup              Office work,
Age 49 Hgt 5-5 3/4 Wgt 155 Color white,Comp-med.
Hair dark-mixed with grey and thin on top, eyes
light hazel, Hat 7-1/4 Shoes No.7-1/2.
Bust 37-1/2 Wst 36-1/2 thigh 21 Neck 14
            Marks & Scars
Head enlarged on the back sticks out, Scar on left
arm near wrist, Dot scar on left shoulderblade.
Long scar on the wrist of right arm, Long scar inside
thumb of left hand, Teeth fairly good.
```

Record of Convict for Peter Lilley. *Colorado State Archives.*

the sinking of the *Titanic*, a small notice indicated that Lilley's application for pardon had been refused the year before but was once again before the pardons board. The article described how the jury had not been aware that each count would result in a separate sentence of some years. "The sentence was the most unheard of thing in the history of the state of Colorado and created a great deal of discussion at the time and since then has constantly been talked about."[78]

Even Judge Shackleford was persuaded to write to the pardons board in favor of paroling Lilley at the end of his first sentence, which would be May 1912.

On May 13, 1912, the parole board commuted the sentence of Peter A. Lilley. Mrs. Lilley went around town thanking everyone who had helped in her campaign to free her husband. On November 7, 1912, Lilley was released on parole. His sentence was discharged April 26, 1918.

The 1920 census shows Peter and Molly Lilley living in Wayne County, Michigan. Sixty-one-year-old Peter was working as a machine operator for a motor company.

MARSHAL JIM CLARK

Though the legend of Jim Clark thrives nowadays, there is surprisingly little reliable information available about the man. What is known is that on August 6, 1895, about midnight, Telluride marshal Jim Clark was walking down Main Street with a friend when someone hiding in the shadows shot him in the chest. Fifty-four-year-old Clark died about an hour later.

By all accounts, there was no real investigation into his assassination, and his killer was never discovered. The rumor was that, for unknown reasons, several prominent Telluride businessmen wanted it that way. Clark's friend, Cyrus Wells "Doc" Shores, the sheriff of Gunnison, was reportedly told to leave town when he asked too many questions after Clark's death.

From Clay County, Missouri, Clark was briefly associated with the notorious Bushwacker William Quantrill as a young man but left after the infamous massacre at Lawrence, Kansas, during which over two hundred men and boys were murdered.

At the time of Clark's death, a *Rocky Mountain News* reporter erroneously claimed that Clark was actually a man named Jim Cummings who made his living robbing trains, stages and banks with the Jesse James and Younger gangs. Cummings later wrote his memoirs and made no mention of Jim Clark.

Clark was also accused of collusion with the McCarty gang who robbed the San Miguel County Bank in 1889. The bandits allegedly paid him that day to make himself scarce. The story is somewhat dubious, however, as Clark wasn't even marshal at the time. Matt Warner, one of the bank robbers, also never mentioned Clark when he wrote his account of the robbery in his memoirs.

Many of the stories about Clark come from the autobiography of Doc Shores. In his eighties when he wrote his memoirs, Shores painted his friend as an outlaw with a heart of gold. Some insist that Shores was simply trying to reconcile the assertions from the *Rocky Mountain News* article with his own fading memories. Shores reported that Clark had a little side business, where he donned a costume, snuck up to the Pandora Road and robbed miners as they traveled to and fro between the town and the mines in the high country. At the same time, Shores said Clark had a soft spot for the needy and was known to help destitute families by lending them money.

One memorable tale from Shores's autobiography is an incident in which a prostitute on Pacific Avenue asked Clark if he would kindly take her aged dog out to a field and put him out of his misery. Clark demonstrated his hatred for prostitutes by pulling his gun and shooting the old pooch on the spot.

Before his death, Clark had reportedly been fired but refused to leave town and made threats against officials. As often seems to be the case where Clark is concerned, there is no corroborating evidence to support this story, and the character and death of Jim Clark remain a mystery to this day.

THE TALE OF THE TREMBLING BANDIT

At mid-afternoon on a hot July day in 1910, stagecoach driver George Brammiere was running the stage from Norwood to Placerville. About eleven miles from Placerville, as he slowed to round a bend, he came upon a man standing in the road. Wearing a mask and pointing a .38 Colt automatic, the man shouted at Brammiere to halt.

As the bandit aimed his pistol at the driver, his arm trembled so violently that the latter feared the gun might go off by accident. The bandit looked to be about twenty-eight, was short with a dark complexion and had the tattered appearance of a hobo, with shabby clothing and a sickly looking physique.

The bandit ordered Brammiere down and directed the passengers to climb out of the coach. The six men lined up at the side of the road, but the bandit seemed so unsure of himself they at first thought it was a joke. The stagecoach passengers included a Montrose insurance agent named Whittle (or Winter); Charles Moritz, a salesman from the J.V. Lathrop hardware store in Montrose; John Kennedy of Denver; Sam Tilden of Norwood; and a young boy named Stone from Bedrock.

The bandit demanded the express box. Brammiere informed him there was no express box on the stage. The shaky fellow settled for the Norwood mail pouch and another unidentified package and then relieved the stagecoach passengers of a total of forty-five dollars, most of it taken from Mr. Kennedy. Throughout the robbery, he waved his gun nervously and kept barking at his victims to "be quick." When he felt he had cleaned them out, he sent the stagecoach along its way. They skedaddled before the weapon could go off due to the fellow's shaking.

The posse used bear hounds to track the trembling bandit. *Special thanks to "Raisin Caine" and Mary Gray of the Vermont Bearhound Association.*

The victims reported that it looked like he had cut his mask from the lining of a coat. He wore it loosely enough that they could see about ten days' growth of beard. He spoke with an accent and seemed to be new at the "sport." They said they could have overwhelmed him had they been carrying weapons. His search for the express box demonstrated inexperience, as stagecoaches did not generally carry those. There was no sign of a horse.

San Miguel County sheriff Tallman put together a posse of local men, including Jack Watson, Harry Prewer and three Galloway brothers of Norwood—John, James and Eugene. James Galloway brought along his celebrated pack of tenacious bear hounds to help with the hunt.

The posse picked up the bandit's trail, which headed into the wilderness and up a mountain to a rocky overlook. There, they discovered where the fellow had sifted through his loot, apparently at some leisure. He had discarded a couple of the purloined items—a man's watch and a lady's waist, or corset, addressed to Mrs. R.M. Beschwitz of Placerville with a return address of Mrs. L.M. McNasser of Redvale. All the mail had been opened and relieved of any money orders or checks. They weren't sure how much the bandit got from the mail pouch but guessed it to be a considerable amount.

The bandit apparently had
no use for the ladies' corset
he found among his loot.
Library of Congress, Prints &
Photographs Division.

From this spot, the posse lost the scent, and they feared the man had escaped into "the wild Tabaguache country."

A week or so later, Sheriff Callaway in Montrose arrested Dan O'Neill on suspicion of the robbery. O'Neill caught the sheriff's attention for several reasons—for one, he was a union man, which at that time was enough to land you on any list of "usual suspects." Plus, he resembled the bandit's description and had also recently been found in the company of a murder suspect in a different case. O'Neill, however, produced an alibi, which had him working in Sawpit at the time of the robbery. His employer verified the story, and he was released.

A year passed without a good suspect, until investigators began focusing on a man the *Telluride Journal* referred to as "one of the most daring desperadoes of the west, sawmill hand and gun man of repute,"[79] Mr. Alexander Peterson. By this time, the story of the robbery had undergone a bewildering transformation. The *Telluride Journal* now declared that the stagecoach had been packed with "hysterical women and frightened men" and that the robbery was "one of the most spectacular in Colorado in years."[80] The formerly trembling bandit was now a bold, heroic fellow menacing folks with a gun in each hand. Though the stage was careening downhill at full speed,

The second version of the bandit amazingly stopped a careening stagecoach by grabbing the lead horses. *Painting by Frederic Remington. Library of Congress, Prints & Photographs Division.*

the amazing man jumped down in front of it, grabbed the lead horses and forced the whole caboodle to an abrupt stop, at which point the vehicle nearly toppled down over a precipice into the great chasm below. The gunman calmly leveled his pistols at the stage, perhaps still holding the horses with his other two hands, and relieved the terrified occupants of all they possessed.

The bandit—presumably Peterson—beat a hasty retreat to "Robbers Roost," an outlaw hangout in Utah. The wily bandit had spent the past year in a cat-and-mouse game with officers hot on his trail who barely missed him at every turn. During this chase, the slippery fellow rode horses to death and tossed bits of his own clothing into the brush so he wouldn't be hampered by it.

In late August 1911, over a year after the stagecoach holdup, the awe-inspiring Alexander Peterson was arrested. A month later, he was released for lack of evidence, and the Norwood stage robbery—both versions of it—remained unsolved.

FOR LOVE OF DIAMONDS

Martin Gabritsch liked shiny things. He especially liked diamonds. He particularly liked something he'd seen on the person of Telluride's popular town druggist and jeweler, Henry C. Baisch—unfortunately for Henry.

Henry C. Baisch was a Telluride institution. For the first two decades of the twentieth century, he operated the H.C. Baisch drug and jewelry store at the corner of Main and Fir Streets. The store was far more than the spot where citizens purchased medicine and other household items or picked out special gifts for their loved ones. Baisch's store also served as a social center for birthday parties, graduation banquets, Easter egg hunts and other community events.

Born in Germany in 1872, Henry (Heinrich) Baisch came to the United States at the age of three with his parents and younger brother. The family first lived in the Dakota Territory and then settled in Nebraska. Young Henry made his appearance in Telluride about 1891, when he went to work as a pharmacist for the local druggist, Johnnie Anderson. In 1898, he set out on his own, buying a partnership in the City Drugstore. In June 1899, he married Eva Munion, and the couple eventually had a daughter and two sons: Vivien, Winfred and Randolph. The popular drugstore eventually became Henry's own, and he developed into one of Telluride's most successful businessmen.

Unfortunately, the store also became a target for bandits. In the early morning hours of October 11, 1908, someone threw several large rocks through the windows of what was then called Baisch & Larson's. The intruder ransacked the place, making off with several bracelets and lavalliere neck chains. As the thief galloped out of town on his horse, a witness recognized him as sixteen-year-old Arthur Narron, who lived up at the Smuggler-Union Mine with his parents.

The sheriff headed up the mountain to the boy's house, where he found the missing jewelry. Much to the dismay of the lad's mother, the sheriff arrested Arthur. Arthur claimed he was drunk and didn't remember any of it. He could not explain the cuts on his hands or the jewelry found in the house. His father volunteered to pay for the considerable damages done to the store.

A much more serious event took place near midnight of June 29, 1921. As Henry Baisch and his clerk closed the store, a man with a gun suddenly appeared out of the darkness. He ordered them to put up their hands. Baisch didn't get his hands up quickly enough, and the man shot him to death.

Posses quickly formed in town, and there was much talk of lynching, as Henry Baisch was a very popular member of the community.

The clerk must have recognized the shooter, because within twenty-four hours, forty-five-year-old Martin Gabritsch of Austria was apprehended at Ophir Loop by two Telluride special deputies, Sam Richards and Jim Penaluna. Gabritsch admitted to his captors that he'd been attracted by Baisch's personal jewelry and could think of no other way of getting the precious gems from Baisch except to hold him up.

On September 9, 1921, an unperturbed Gabritsch pleaded guilty at his preliminary hearing. He was reported to have a "coolness almost amounting to effrontery."[81] Refusing the services of an attorney, he said he had $2,200 in the bank but preferred that "mein brudters und sisters can have de money."[82] A trial was set for November to determine whether he would get a life sentence or death by hanging.

In late October, Gabritsch's plea still stood at "guilty," but the question of his sanity had become an issue. He was examined by a Denver alienist (psychologist), Dr. Edward Delehanty. In his report, Delehanty stated that "Gabritsch was of very low mentality, but not sufficiently low to excuse him from responsibility for the crime of murdering Mr. Baisch."[83] Gabritsch's head was covered with scars, which the psychologist seemed to regard as significant. Rumors circulated that Gabritsch had the nickname around Telluride as "Crazy Martin" and that he had a "mania for diamonds."[84] Delehanty recommended life in prison.

District court opened Monday, November 12, 1921, and Martin Gabritsch was now defended by prominent Ouray attorney Carl Sigfrid. The courtroom was packed with friends and sympathizers of Baisch from all around the district, although the threat of lynching had dissipated.

Gabritsch was markedly changed on his day in court. He was described as a broken man in a "pitiable condition." "His naturally ruddy complexion had paled to an almost dead white and he swayed constantly in his chair with a peculiar, dog-like motion. His jaws worked as though he were chewing and there was a muscular twitching in his neck."[85]

Gabritsch's motive for killing Baisch was an "unreasonable craving for the possession for diamonds and his desire to own one which Baisch constantly wore."[86] In a rather unique situation, both the prosecution and the defense urged the jury to return a sentence of life in prison. The jurors left to deliberate, taking a dinner break at the Sheridan to continue their discussion in a private booth. Three hours later, they returned to the courtroom with their sentence.

Before reading the verdict, Judge Straud M. Logan asked Gabritsch if he had anything to say. Gabritsch stood up and pulled out a sheet of paper, from which he read his prepared statement: "I'm guilty. Not responsible. I sorry. Please give me short sentence."[87] The jury did not give him "short sentence." They gave him life at hard labor in the state penitentiary.

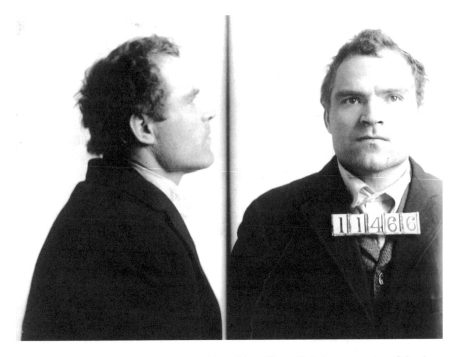

Martin Gabritsch was attracted to some shiny objects Henry Baisch was wearing. *Colorado State Archives.*

Martin Gabritsch 11466 received from San Miguel
Co., 11-23-21 for Murder under LIFE sentence. Age ther
35; Wgtxk 165; Hgt. 5-6 7/8; Sallow complxn. Bust 38;
Waist 35; Thigh 18; Neck 15; Hat 7; Shoes 9; Med. Brov
hair; Gray-Brown eyes; Med. build; Male; Austrian; bor
in Austria; lived in Colo. 10 yrs; in U.S. 10 yrs. Oc-
cupation- Quartz Miner. Marks & Scars: Scar L bk head
2 scars lower bk. head; scar L 4head; scar L cheek; sc
R upper lip; 4 scars bk. neck; Tatoos: "Geb 1836 A 190
-1910"; Mermaid & Anchor- L upper arm; Hand & Bouquet
of flowers- bk. L 4arm; "Die Schonde Liebs"; wreath, 2
hearts, anchor & dagger- front L 4arm; Ladies head &
bust, 2 ferns- front L wrist; "K.V.K. Infanterie Regi-
ment Freicher, von Succowati No. 87.11.Feld Hompagnic,
in Pola 1907-1910", Austrian Eagle, M Maltese-cross G
wreath- front R 4arm; Austrian Coat of Arms- on chest,
scar bk. L wrist; 2 Vax R U arm; scar bk. R hand; scar
R kneecap; 2 scars L back. Friend-- Paul Nardin, Tell
uride, Colo.
Finger Print Class'n,......

Record of Convict for Martin Gabritsch. *Colorado State Archives.*

On November 23, after Gabritsch had spent almost five months in the county jail, Telluride deputies escorted the killer to Cañon City, where he spent the rest of his life.

The following month, Sheriff George G. Wagner "netted a nice sum" by selling the property of Martin Gabritsch to the highest bidder, hoping to recoup the expense of his prosecution. Items that fetched a total of $275 included "1 trunk, 2 suit cases, 1 suit of clothes, 1 overcoat, 2 gold watches, 1 locket, 2 stick pins, 2 watch chains, 2 pair cuff buttons, 1 ring, 1 compass."[88]

TELLURIDE'S GUNFIGHTER-
DEPUTY, BOB MELDRUM

In the early days of Telluride's decade-long mine labor troubles, the Telluride Businessmen's Association brought two gun-slinging "enforcers" to town to help "discourage" the union. One of those was Robert D. "Bob" Meldrum. Meldrum was a shadowy figure with a sour, boozy reputation. Rumors circulated that he had killed over a dozen men, though there isn't any evidence to support that legend. Born in 1866 in England, Meldrum came to the United States in 1880. After deputies snagged him in possession of saddles from some stolen horses, he served a prison sentence in Montana from December 13, 1894, to August 18, 1896.[89]

Sometime during the 1890s, he befriended the infamous Tom Horn, a Pinkerton gunslinger who was suspected of assassinating a number of men he deemed to be cattle rustlers. Horn was later hanged for shooting the young son of one such cattleman.

Meldrum's own gun slinging first brought him notice in Wyoming newspapers in 1900 when he was deputy sheriff of Dixon, Wyoming. In November, he shot and killed a man named Noah Wilkerson. Wilkerson was a married Texas ranchman and father of nine who was wanted for murder. He had escaped from a Texas jail and had been on the run for about five months when he wandered into Meldrum's territory.

On Wednesday, November 4, 1900, Meldrum took notice of the fellow and thought he might be the fugitive Wilkerson. He later testified that he spent the day with Wilkerson to make sure he had the right man. After the two ate dinner together, Meldrum announced to Wilkerson that he was under arrest. Wilkerson resisted, and the two struggled over Wilkerson's rifle.

Robert D. "Bob" Meldrum and his gunslinger kit. *Library of Congress, Prints & Photographs Division.*

When the rifle fell to the ground, Wilkerson pulled his six-shooter. Meldrum beat him to the draw and shot him in the mouth.

This story raised some eyebrows later when the county physician reported that Wilkerson had actually been shot in the back, with the bullet leaving his body through the mouth.[90] Despite this discrepancy, Meldrum was congratulated on the "capture" of Wilkerson and given a nice reward.

A year later, in 1901, Meldrum arrived in Telluride and went to work for the Telluride Businessmen's Association along with another hired gun, Willard Runnels. There, Meldrum married a woman named Cora Morgan, who was thirteen years his junior.

Meldrum's initial instructions were to patrol the town at night and keep a low profile but to let union members know he was there. He and Runnels were soon given more official positions as deputies under Sheriff Cal Rutan, whose actions had often demonstrated his loyalty to the mine owners and Telluride Businessmen's Association.

On November 23, 1903, during the millworkers strike, five strikers were "parading about the Tomboy mill and grounds armed with rifles and revolvers, threatening men who anticipated going to work and making other riotous demonstrations. They jumped on Geo. Nixon, forbid him going to work, and made threats against him in the event of his going to work."[91] Meldrum arrested the men and sent for Runnels to escort them down the mountain to jail in town. The *Telluride Journal* gleefully reported how the men were marched all the way down the mountain from the Tomboy Mine into Telluride:

> *The men were "hog-tied," their arms being fastened close to their legs by ropes about the wrist, then they were tied together and the rope attached to Deputy Runnell's [sic] saddle horn, and in that way they were marched down the trail. When the arrests were made one of the gang succeeded in escaping, but he was afterwards arrested in town. It is proposed to hold these agitators in jail, and there are others who will join them if they are not more guarded in their actions and utterances than they have been.*
>
> *The time for exciting men to anarchy and creating disturbances is past in Telluride.*[92]

In April 1904, Meldrum was doing double duty as a Telluride deputy and a guard for the Tomboy. His reputation as an anti-union hired gun and his heavy-handed enforcement of anti-alcohol regulations on mining property had earned him many enemies among the miners. Reportedly, Meldrum was a big drinker himself and was often seen drunk.

On April 2, Meldrum had a fatal run-in with a fifty-five-year-old miner named Olaf Tissel (or Thissell). Tissel had a reputation as a good worker but was also a heavy drinker, and it came out later that he had been in prison twice, including once for stabbing a man. He had tangled with Tomboy guards in the past and was once hospitalized with delirium tremens.

On this occasion, Tissel showed up drunk at the supper table. Later, when the men were lounging in a sitting room, Meldrum approached Tissel and asked him where he got the whiskey. Tissel replied that it was none of his damn business. Meldrum shoved the man's coat aside and searched his pockets for the bottle. Tissel didn't care for that, so he head-butted Meldrum. Meldrum staggered, recovered and lunged after Tissel, but a man named O'Brien grabbed Meldrum's wrists, and Tissel head-butted the latter again. Meldrum wrenched away from O'Brien, pulled his gun and shot Tissel dead.

Several of the regional papers took sides, based on their stance in the labor strife. The anti-union *Telluride Journal* reported that it was a setup, the intent being to "get" Meldrum. Meldrum later made statements to that effect. The pro-union *Durango Democrat* reported, "Since the tragedy occurred a big crowd of men have quit the Tomboy Mine saying no quarrel had existed and no justice could be gotten if ever such thing should happen again, 'therefore we quit.' Others who know too much have been discharged."[93] Another pro-union newspaper, the *Ouray Plaindealer*, had a similar take on the killing:

> *The Denver Post arrived Sunday, with its characteristic tendency to malign and slander any workingman, justifies the killing of the miner, stating that he had brought whisky to the mine, and had engaged in a scuffle with Meldrum. The editor of Plaindealer talked with a party of Tom Boy miners on the east bound train Sunday, who witnessed the whole affair, and from their statements in detail is forced to the conclusion that it was nothing short of a cold blooded murder. The deputy, Meldrum, accused the miner, a Sweede [sic], named Ole Tissel, of having whisky about him, and attempted to search him. To this the miner objected, and a scuffle ensued, during which Meldrum drew a revolver and shot the man dead in his tracks. The workman was unarmed. Meldrum is now out on bond, furnished by the Tom Boy management. He is a hired thug, bad man and a killer imported by the Tom Boy company for purpose of intimidation, a former confederate of Tom Horn.*[94]

Meldrum was arrested for the shooting, arraigned before Justice Peter A. Lilley (of future embezzlement fame) and then released on a $10,000 bond. The coroner held an inquest, and the jury ruled that Tissel "came to his death by a shot fired by Robert Meldrum and 'that said shot was fired in the heat of passion with felonious intent.'"[95]

The trial was scheduled for the May term in district court, the period during which Telluride was under martial law. When District Court Judge Stevens was greeted at the train station by troops searching his train for deported union miners, he angrily cancelled the court session, saying:

> [Our] *constitution provides that the military shall always be in strict subordination to the civil authorities.*
>
> *It is doubtless construed differently, however, by the Executive* [Governor Peabody], *who has declared this County to be in the state of insurrection and has declared martial law within its limits. In effect, therefore, the Executive has said that there is no law in this County except the military commander.*[96]

Meanwhile, Meldrum had other business to take care of, since the two head-butts from Tissel had knocked out some of his teeth: "Mr. Meldrum will go to Denver within a day or two to receive dental treatment, his teeth loosened by the bunts given him, being held in position by small gold wires. It is hoped that by scientific treatment the loosened teeth will be preserved, and encouraged to attach themselves by fresh roots."[97]

While in Denver getting his "fresh roots," Meldrum thrilled eager newspaper reporters with an embellished version of the killing that centered on the "conspiracy" to do him in: "I am bound to make enemies," said he. "Anyone is in my position. It was a put-up job, this Tissel thing. Tissel was to pick a fight, and then his partner was to hold me while the other fellow put me out of business. I simply was a little too quick with my trigger—that was the only obstacle to carrying out the scheme."[98]

Bob Meldrum was eventually acquitted of the shooting. Years later, in 1912, the *Telluride Journal* was faithfully reporting an even more enhanced version of Meldrum's conspiracy theory: "It was claimed that Thistle [*sic*] and a companion went to the Tomboy to secure employment with the declared intention of killing Meldrum."[99]

In September 1904, Meldrum lived at Ptarmigan Lake, where he was in charge of watching for union members who had been "deported" out of Telluride and preventing them from sneaking back into town from Ouray. Around that time, Fort Peabody was built at the summit of Imogene Pass, serving as a stone outpost and sniper nest that would allow more permanent sentries to keep the "undesirables" out.

On November 24, 1904, Meldrum was appointed deputy city marshal of Telluride, but he lasted less than six months in that position. Over the next few years, he bounced back and forth between serving as a guard for the Tomboy and working as an agent for the Pinkerton detective agency.

In 1906, he was recruited by the Pinkertons to help with a bizarre plot to kidnap three prominent union officials and bring them to Idaho to face charges in the murder of former governor Frank Steunenberg. Harry Orchard, who got a life sentence for the murder, claimed that he had committed the deed at the behest of WFM president Charles Moyer, Secretary Bill Haywood and former union officer George Pettibone.

Later, during the trial itself, Meldrum served as bodyguard for the prosecution. All three union men were acquitted. Haywood and Pettibone were defended by famed defense attorney Clarence Darrow.

In between jobs for the Pinkertons, Meldrum returned to Telluride, heading immediately up to Ptarmigan Lake, which seemed to serve as a refuge for him. He was even reported to have thrown a "dance party" for friends up at the lake.

Deported union men sneaking back into Telluride would have traveled this stage road between Ouray and Silverton. *Library of Congress, Prints & Photographs Division.*

On November 17, 1907, Meldrum was involved in another shooting at the Tomboy company store in Savage Basin. The trouble began at ten or eleven o'clock at night during what began as a friendly dice game inside the store. A man named David Lambert had been on a drinking binge for several days. On the night of the seventeenth, the watchman at the Tomboy boardinghouse had escorted the drunken fellow to his bed several times, the

William Pinkerton in his office in 1904. He was the son of founder Allan Pinkerton.
Library of Congress, Prints & Photographs Division.

Left to right: George Pettibone, Bill Haywood and Charles Moyer outside the Boise, Idaho sheriff's office awaiting trial for allegedly murdering ex-governor Frank Steunenberg.
Library of Congress, Prints & Photographs Division.

last time waiting while the latter undressed and climbed into bed. However, Lambert soon appeared in the company store, wearing nothing but slippers and an undershirt beneath his coat. Witnesses said he was extremely intoxicated. A friend of Lambert's, Dennis Curtin, began teasing him about playing a game of pool, reportedly hoping that he could beat Lambert for once, as Lambert was well known as an excellent pool player.

The teasing escalated into a tussle. The night guard on duty, Thomas Sullivan, came in. Another good friend of Dennis Curtin's, he told the men not to fight and physically intervened, whereupon Lambert pulled a gun and shot him three times. Sullivan staggered out the door and fell on the platform outside. Lambert stepped over him and ran off.

Sullivan managed to fire at Lambert as the latter made his escape, but there were conflicting accounts as to whether he hit him. Some witnesses said that Sullivan missed his mark and that Dennis Curtin picked up Sullivan's gun and shot at Lambert, giving him two flesh wounds.

After Lambert disappeared, several men ran to Meldrum's place and woke him up. Meldrum got up, packed his gun and went looking for Lambert. While Meldrum searched along on the road, others at the mill spotted Lambert sneaking into the "Little Vanner Room" at the Tomboy mill. Meldrum entered the mill, where a bookkeeper and another man were working. Meldrum spotted Lambert and told him to put up his hands. Lambert reportedly made a move with his hands, and Meldrum shot and killed him.

The "dead wagon" came along and carried both men down into town. Bill Sullivan was alive and was taken to the hospital in Durango, where doctors operated on him for nine hours. The bullets had made over a dozen perforations in Sullivan's intestines, which the doctors sewed up. The next morning, Sullivan was awake and talking with friends, but most did not expect him to live.

Lambert's body had three bullet wounds in it: in his right forearm, his right hip and a fatal wound in his liver. Friends of Lambert said they had never known him to carry a gun and could not say where he got the weapon.

Lambert was about thirty-five years old, from Idaho and performed a difficult and dangerous job at the Tomboy as a trammer—one who pushes ore carts to the mine opening. Like Olaf Tissel, he was known to have a drinking problem.

Thomas Sullivan was originally from Cork, Ireland, and was good friends with Dennis Curtin and his brother Tim, a shift boss at the Tomboy. The Curtins were also from the Cork area. Sullivan had only been in Telluride for a few months after working as a longshoreman in New York City for nearly ten years.

The day after the shootings, Telluride sheriff Fitzpatrick traveled up to the Tomboy and arrested Bob Meldrum. On November 19, the coroner's jury ruled that Lambert had died from a gunshot wound at the hands of Meldrum but could not yet determine whether it was with felonious intent or not. That same day, Bill Sullivan died of his wounds.

A few days later, Lambert's brother arrived in town to take his body back to Keokuk, Iowa. (In a tragic coincidence, the brother contracted pneumonia during this trip and died himself soon after.)

Meldrum, meanwhile, waived his preliminary hearing. His benefactors, Bulkeley Wells and a couple others, quickly paid his bail, and he left town for Ptarmigan Lake. In May 1908, Bob Meldrum went on trial for murder. His defense was that Lambert had just killed someone and that he couldn't take any chances with the fellow. The two witnesses corroborated Meldrum's story of the shooting. After deliberating for a little over an hour, the jury found him not guilty of murder in the death of David Lambert.

A week later, he left his job at the Tomboy. He also left Telluride and headed to Norwood, where he had landed a contract to work for a year as a "ranger" for the San Miguel County Stock Growers' Association. There had been plenty of recent trouble with cattle rustlers, and the cattlemen hoped that Meldrum's presence on the range would intimidate any further mischief-makers. However, there was considerable grumbling among cowboys about sharing the range with a known gunman—particularly someone who had recently killed a man. For unknown reasons, Meldrum's tenure in that job ended after about a month. In June, the *Telluride Journal* reported that Meldrum had "gone fishing" and that his wife would remain in Telluride. Upon his return, Meldrum was back up at Ptarmigan Lake. An August 28, 1908 report in the *Journal* describes a pleasant visit that two Telluride men made to Meldrum at his home at Ptarmigan Lake, during which they went sailing.

That fall, Meldrum and his wife again left Telluride, this time moving back to Baggs, Wyoming, where he went to work for the Snake River Cattlemen's Association. Meldrum wrote to his friends in Telluride in November of that year, boasting that the citizens of Baggs had made him a deputy sheriff because of his "wholesome influence" on the "red necks" in their area.[100] He was also doing double duty as an enforcer for the big cattlemen. These men reportedly believed that "most of the homesteaders who have taken out small ranches along the Little Snake Valley and its vicinity are not legitimate ranchmen, but are cattle rustlers, who pass on the stolen stock into Wyoming and Utah…It is to break up this system that Bob Meldrum has been called upon."[101]

On January 19, 1912, Meldrum had become marshal of Baggs when he added another notch to his belt. Conflicting stories emerged about the shooting, but according to outraged witnesses, a popular local cowboy named Chick Bowen was doing nothing but standing in front of a Baggs hotel yelling when Meldrum shot him. Apparently, yelling (or "whooping it up") was against a town ordinance.

Meldrum was arrested on charges of first-degree murder. "Cowboys and citizens of Baggs" raised money to fund the prosecution, while Meldrum's defense was paid for by "several wealthy men in Southern Wyoming."[102]

The trial, held in November 1912, ended with a hung jury. For his second trial, over fifty witnesses from the valley of the Snake River were called to testify.[103] On August 25, 1913, the jury convicted him of murder in the second degree, and he was sentenced to twenty-one to thirty-five years in prison. His attorneys appealed the conviction all the way to the Wyoming Supreme Court. On April 15, 1915, the court set aside his conviction, ordered his third trial and released Meldrum on bail.[104]

Meldrum decided he wasn't going to hang around for the latest trial. Scheduled for February 14, 1916, the trial date arrived and Meldrum was nowhere to be found. He had skipped out on his $18,000 bond and disappeared. About a month later, he wrote to Sheriff Rivera of Rawlins that he was in New York and wanted to turn himself in.

On June 28, 1916, after a change of venue from Rawlins to Cheyenne, Bob Meldrum had his third trial. He was found guilty of manslaughter and sentenced to five to seven years in the penitentiary at Rawlins, Wyoming. His attorney had appealed for leniency because of the stress Meldrum had undergone during the previous four years since the shooting.[105] A motion for a new trial was denied, and Bob Meldrum was escorted to the Wyoming State Penitentiary.

In the summer of 1917, after a little over a year in prison, Meldrum was released on parole. He was later pardoned.

DOC MENTZER AND THE MYSTERIOUS MONROES

B orn in Sweden in 1864, Dr. Oscar F. Mentzer immigrated to the United States in 1881. By 1890, he had become a physician in his new country, setting up shop on Larimer Street in Denver. He enjoyed a reputation as a skilled surgeon and built up a large practice reportedly worth $15,000 per year. Mentzer was also known as a charitable, kind doctor who treated many poor patients without charge. His partner in Denver, a pharmacist named S.A. Gross, told the *Telluride Journal* that Dr. Mentzer

> *was absolutely the best physician I ever knew, both in diagnosis and in prescribing for the complaint. The first year he was here he sent an average of 20 subscriptions a day into the store; my books show it. That meant an income for him of at least $60 a day.*
>
> *His reputation spread and people came from all over Colorado, from Kansas and Nebraska, and one couple from Utah to consult him. He was no specialist, treated all diseases. He stood well with the other doctors here.*[106]

While living in Denver, Mentzer stayed at the Hotel Albert. There, he met Emma May Monroe, who had come to Colorado from Chicago for health reasons. On July 24, 1894, Oscar and Emma went to Colorado Springs, where they were married. He later described his love for her as a "worshipping" love.[107] Emma was described as "a handsome woman and very devoted to her husband."[108] Except for the salacious details that came out later, little is known about Emma May Monroe's background.

Unfortunately, despite his happy circumstances, thirty-year-old Dr. Mentzer was an alcoholic. His drinking soon began to interfere with his practice. He missed days in the office and patients left his care, seeking a more sober physician. Within a year or two of their marriage, Emma Mentzer left her husband and returned to Chicago, where she reportedly divorced him.

Mentzer was aware of his problem. After his wife left him, he announced to his friends and remaining patients that he was getting away from the temptations of the city and moving out to the country, intending to reform himself. In January 1897, Dr. Mentzer moved to Telluride, where he set up a new practice.

For the next year or so, local papers were dotted with brief items about "Doc Mentzer's" work with the community: bringing new babies into the world, nursing children with pneumonia back to health, repairing someone's shattered arm and helping a miner recover from a dislocated hip. He was generally respected around town as a "very able surgeon." However, there were some incidents where "he committed acts that did not meet with general approval...and he was feared to a certain extent, especially by female patients."[109]

During this period—apparently toward the end of 1897—he heard from his ex-wife "that she was sick and starving and imposed upon, and that if she didn't have [Doc Mentzer] she would have to starve to death."[110] From November 1897 to August 1898, Doc Mentzer continuously sent money to Emma, up to $900 during 1898. Depending on the formula used, this calculates to anywhere between $24,000 and $709,000 in today's dollars.[111] In his correspondence with Emma during this period, Oscar reportedly begged her to come back to him, promising that he had quit drinking for good. Emma finally agreed. In July 1898, Mentzer met her in Denver. There, they reconciled and reportedly remarried, though no records exist of the remarriage. (It's also possible they never actually divorced.) On August 2, 1898, Doc Mentzer returned to Telluride, surprising his neighbors by bringing with him a "bride."

Although Emma reportedly returned to Doc Mentzer only because he had sobered up, others insisted he was not sober. Around the time when Oscar and Emma reconciled, Mentzer also sought out his former partner in Denver, the pharmacist S.A. Gross. Gross later told the *Telluride Journal*: "Mentzer was here in Denver six weeks or so ago. He wanted to come back with me again but I told him no. He was too far gone. He looked seedy from drinking so much. He said he was going to stop drinking for good, but I could see he'd never be again the man he had been, so I wouldn't have him."[112]

Emma's brother, Will Monroe, also moved to Telluride at the same time, bringing his wife with him. A marine engineer, he was planning to go to work at the Bessie Mill as a maintenance man on the engines and boilers. The couple stayed with the Mentzers.

During the first week of October, Mentzer visited the Tompkins Hardware Company in Telluride and purchased a .32-caliber Iver Johnson pistol. He told the salesman that he needed protection against "dogs and holdups"[113] when he traveled at night to places like Sawpit. The salesman later insisted that Doc Mentzer was perfectly sober when he purchased the weapon or he would not have sold it to him.

According to Will Monroe's account, on October 7, the two couples passed a pleasant evening together, and the doctor was jovial and smiling. About 9:30 in the evening, Emma suddenly called to her brother from another room. Just as he arrived to see what she wanted, he heard a scream and a shot. As he entered the room, the doctor turned toward him, a smoking gun in his hand. Monroe grabbed Mentzer and wrestled him for the gun. Monroe got it away from the doctor and tossed it to his wife, who threw it out into the yard. Monroe and Mentzer—both "splendid specimens of physical manhood"[114]—continued fighting. Monroe soon had the upper hand and beat the doctor until the latter was unconscious. He then dragged Mentzer out to the porch and threw him into a heap.

Monroe returned to the house and only then discovered that his sister had been shot in the temple. Emma Mentzer died about half an hour later. When officials arrived, they found the doctor unconscious on the porch.

Mentzer was carried to the sheriff's office, where he remained unconscious on a cot in the corridor. Crowds soon gathered, and talk of lynching circulated, but no action was taken. His jailers believed that Mentzer was shamming and did not call a doctor for him. The *San Miguel Examiner* expressed great dismay over Mrs. Mentzer's death: "Mrs. Mentzer was a most charming and amiable woman and possessed the traits that made her lovable to all, and her sad fate brings great sorrow to her relatives and the community alike."[115]

The next day it became evident that Mentzer had a serious head injury, and the sheriff called for help. Doctors Hall and Clark could not bring him around and announced they would have to trepan his skull (drill a hole) to relieve the pressure. Although the doctors weren't optimistic about Mentzer's survival, he pulled through. While in his jail sickbed, he received constant care from a fellow inmate, an artist named John Brooke. Imprisoned for uttering (cashing a forged check), Brooke had previously gained attention because of the lovely oil paintings he left on the walls of Sheriff Downtain's offices, including a rendition of a string of speckled trout.[116]

The day after the shooting, two investigators searching the yard of Mentzer's house found the Iver Johnson pistol out in the grass where Monroe's wife had thrown it. The revolver had a capacity of five shells, and there were four unexploded shells in the gun, along with one empty cartridge. This fact tended to corroborate Monroe's story that there had been only one shot; however, Mentzer later insisted that the shell had only "half exploded" and that the same shell's second explosion during the struggle with Monroe was the one that killed his wife.

The coroner's inquest concluded that Dr. Mentzer had shot his wife with felonious intent. A couple days later, Emma Mentzer's body was carried to the depot by a group of men and put on the train back to her home in Chicago. The *San Miguel Examiner* declared that "[t]his mad act has cast a gloom over the entire city and will go down as one of the most deplorable and atrocious acts in the varied history of San Miguel County."[117]

Mentzer gradually came out of his coma and could sit up, but he was still swollen beyond recognition. When the subject of the shooting came up, he became so agitated that Sheriff Downtain forbade folks from talking about it in the doctor's presence.

Eventually, Mentzer hired a defense attorney, John G. Taylor, a well-respected lawyer with a reputation for eloquence. The Swedish community in town contributed generously to Mentzer's defense. However, stories were already circulating around town about the doctor's dissipation and fall from the heights of success he had enjoyed in Denver. After interviewing his former partner, Gross, the *Telluride Journal* offered this assessment of the doctor:

> *Physicians now practicing here* [in Denver] *who remember Dr. Mentzer confirm what Mr. Gross says of his skill. He seemed to have a natural faculty for diagnosis, seeming to know instinctively the nature of the patient's trouble. He was an unwearying watcher at a patient's bedside for he could not bear to lose a case. His habit, it is said, was, when he considered a case hopeless, to get drunk and forget about it. His old friends were amazed when they heard that he had murdered his wife when drunk. The effect of alcohol on him as they had observed him was to make him very genial and very happy and very comical.*[118]

Finally, Mentzer gathered his wits enough to tell his story to a reporter. During the interview, his head was still swathed in bandages, and his emotional state swung back and forth between sadness and agitation. He claimed he had bought the revolver for his wife, not for himself. He said she asked for the gun, feeling that she needed protection because he was gone so often at night.

On the evening of the shooting, according to Mentzer, he sat down in a rocking chair to show his wife how to operate the gun. During this process, the gun went off accidentally but did not hit anything. (Interestingly, the *Journal* first reported that a bullet was found in the wall but said later that there was no sign of bullet holes in the walls of the home.) When the gun went off, Mentzer stood up at the moment his brother-in-law ran into the room. Monroe, mistakenly assuming Mentzer was trying to kill Emma, jumped on Mentzer and began to muscle the gun away. Mentzer insisted that Emma was shot by accident:

> *Of course I had no time to explain to him as he jumped right onto me and grabbed hold of the gun which I was holding in my left hand and the pressure of his hand over mine on the gun caused it to explode again and it was then that my wife was shot. Where the bullet struck her I do not know, but should say from the way the gun was held, it would strike her in the face.*
>
> *I had no chance to explain as he would not stop to listen and if he had there would have been no shot fired the second time, as the force of his hand on the gun over my hand caused me to pull the trigger, and he kept beating me fearfully…*
>
> *If I had intended to commit murder or suicide I never would have trusted a .32 caliber gun to do anything like that. And why should I even think of trying to murder the woman I loved and I know loved me? I might as well be dead too, for I have nothing to live for now.*[119]

Mentzer pointed out that he'd been holding the gun in his left hand at the time and that he wouldn't have tried to shoot with his left hand since he was right-handed.

The *Telluride Journal* published a notice the next day about Mentzer's statement:

> *Mentzer is well on the road to recovery but the doctors say he is not yet out of danger. He himself says he is all right and seems confident of gaining his liberty as soon as the matter is understood.*
>
> *His earnest manner created a deep impression on the minds of all who heard the statement. Whether it is the hallucination of a mind diseased, the*

truth, or lies, is a matter for the courts to determine. At any rate, there should be no hasty action, and there will be none. Let the law decide.[120]

Three weeks after the shooting, Mentzer had his preliminary hearing. The only witnesses, Will Monroe and his wife, gave mixed and contradictory testimony during this hearing, and observers began to express doubts about their reliability and respectability. The *Journal* reported rumors that the defense had information that would shed new light on the case. A week before the trial began in early December, another story circulated that the star witnesses would not be around: "There was a great stirring about this morning before daylight, looking for the sleeping rooms of attorneys and court officers. Some of the officers detailed to keep an eye on the witnesses in the Mentzer case got an idea that an important witness was preparing to take the early train."[121]

Mr. and Mrs. Monroe did stay in town, one way or another, and on December 2, the jury was seated and the trail got underway. The case was a sensational one for Telluride, and the courtroom was packed with the curious, with many more being turned away.

Testimony began with several neighbors of the Mentzers, who said that they heard a shot and screams and ran over to see what happened. One of the neighbors, a Mr. Adams, had taken it upon himself to measure the powder burns around the bullet hole in Mrs. Mentzer's temple, which he found to be one and a half inches in diameter. Another neighbor, Mrs. Cleveland, declared on the stand that the Mentzers quarreled constantly.

Will Monroe then took the witness stand. He was described as "an intelligent appearing man, uses good language, and though visibly affected while reciting the details of the murder, told a straight story that impressed the jury and audience."[122]

The story that Monroe told at the trial did not match the story he originally told police—that Doc Mentzer had been on a lengthy drinking binge and Emma was nursing him through a hangover. On the stand, he said nothing about a binge. He stated that on the evening of the shooting, Mentzer went to bed at 8:30 p.m. but then came back out around 9:00. After that, Monroe and his wife went outside and soon heard Emma call out Will's name. He ran into the room and saw the doctor and his sister standing and the doctor's arm raised. Emma screamed, the gun went off and Emma fell. Monroe jumped on Mentzer. As the men struggled, Mentzer "mumbled something, the effect of which I could not understand, but the last portion of which was, 'I had to do it, and I will kill you, too, because you are the cause of all my troubles.'"[123] Monroe also testified that during their struggle, Mentzer told him that the gun was filled with blank cartridges and that Mentzer said "he fired the gun only to scare her."[124]

When Mentzer's attorney, John Taylor, began questioning Monroe, it quickly became apparent that he intended to discredit the witness. He shocked the courtroom by announcing that the woman Monroe referred to as his wife was not his wife at all. The prosecution objected vehemently, and as it was nearly ten o'clock at night, the court adjourned.

In the morning, the attorneys argued for a couple hours about whether the character of Will Monroe should be an issue in the trial. The defense declared that Monroe had abandoned his real wife and children in Chicago and that this fact had a bearing on his reliability as a witness. Finally, the judge ruled in favor of the prosecution, saying, "People might be living in unlawful relations and still their evidence on the witness stand would be entitled to full credence."[125] The testimony of "Mr. and Mrs." Monroe ended up being much shorter than planned, as the defense attorney could not pursue that line of questioning.

Finally, Doc Mentzer got on the stand and told his version of the events. He performed well under questioning from his own attorney, but Attorney Hogg, the prosecutor, managed to muddle him up and cause him to lose his previous aura of quiet dignity. The *Journal* wrote: "His answers impressed one as coming from a witness in a trance; one with a very imperfect appreciation of the occurrence being inquired into."[126]

Despite his "trance," Mentzer's testimony deviated little from what he had already told the reporter, insisting that he had no desire to shoot his wife and that the gun had gone off by accident during his struggle with Monroe.

When the examinations were complete, the prosecution and defense made lengthy summaries, with Taylor living up to his reputation as an elegant speaker. At mid-afternoon, the jury retired to deliberate. Discussions lasted for nineteen hours, through the night.

The courtroom was packed on the early morning of December 5, 1898, when the jury announced the verdict: they found Doc Mentzer guilty of murder in the second degree, with a recommendation for leniency. The judge sentenced Mentzer to twenty years of hard labor in the penitentiary. Members of the jury later told reporters that all agreed the doctor had shot his wife but they argued over the degree of guilt.

After the trial, public opinion swung sharply in Mentzer's favor when details emerged about the questionable character of the Monroes, including Emma. On December 5, 1898, Will Monroe's real wife arrived in town, having traveled all the way from Illinois. It turned out that she and her attorneys had been scouring the country looking for Monroe, and headlines about the shooting had revealed his whereabouts. Mrs. Tessa Monroe spoke at some length with folks at the *Journal*, who reported that

> *she* [the real Mrs. Monroe] *has lived with relatives since being deserted in Chicago last spring, and left penniless with three small children to care for.*
>
> *She is an intelligent, refined, ladylike woman, of very pleasing manners. The JOURNAL had a long interview with her, and she tells a story of outrage and inhuman treatment at the hands of Monroe, in a straightforward, simple manner, that carries conviction, and makes the listeners' blood boil with indignation.*
>
> *She was married to Monroe in 1893, and has three small children. Her life with him, for several years past, she says has been extremely unpleasant. Two years ago, at Cleveland, the officers of the humane society took the family in charge, put Monroe under bonds to preserve the peace and for months watched over her and the children, forcing Monroe to provide them with food and fuel.*[127]

Mrs. Monroe said that her husband had beaten and strangled her on many occasions. Finally, he took her and the children to her sister's house in Chicago and left them there. After many weeks without word, she hired detectives to hunt him down. They found him in a Chicago bordello with the woman he now claimed as his wife. She stated further that Emma Mentzer, formerly Emma Monroe, had been the "landlady" of the Chicago bordello and at that time was in court facing charges of theft. The Monroes all took off, and that was the last Mrs. Monroe knew of them until she read in the papers about the shooting in Telluride. During her conversation with the *Journal*, Mrs. Monroe presented letters from officials in Chicago substantiating her claims.

The *Journal* summarized its latest take on the Mentzer affair:

> *The whole history of her (Mrs. Monroe's) life with Monroe shows him to be a most despicable character, and it is a little remarkable that the proven bigamist and self confessed perjurer should be allowed to quietly slip away without punishment. His sister, whose evil influence it seems had much to do with his downfall and his outrageous treatment of his wife and children, and their final abandonment, is in her grave, sent there by a bullet fired by the man she had driven to frenzy.*[128]

The paper also reported that "Mrs. Monroe…is a very charming little woman; and several of the susceptible beaux about the New Sheridan were hopeful that she would remain and get a divorce from Monroe."[129]

By that time, Will Monroe and his other "wife" had disappeared from Telluride, apparently forgoing his job at the Bessie. The last anyone heard of him was a report that "Mrs. Monroe number one is now in Denver, where she has put the police on the trail of her bigamist husband."[130]

Within a week of Mentzer's conviction, word got out that the murder case might be reopened or appealed to a higher court. Mentzer had influential friends among the Swedish community in Denver, and they were mobilizing on his behalf. Meanwhile, on December 8, 1898, Sheriff Downtain escorted Doc Mentzer to Cañon City.

A model prisoner, Mentzer worked in the dispensary. He reportedly had a bad leg, possibly from Monroe's beating, and he had trouble sleeping. For this, he took chloral hydrate. In July 1900, notices appeared in several papers that his friends and attorney were working on a getting him a pardon.

About twenty months after beginning his sentence, on August 16, 1900, Doc Mentzer showed up in the prison kitchen asking for coffee. Before he could take a sip, the doctor fell to the floor and died. They soon discovered that he had taken an overdose of chloral hydrate.

Officials speculated that he had committed suicide, but others argued that he had been hopeful about getting a pardon. Those present on the scene pointed out that he seemed to be trying to get the coffee because he knew he had taken too much of the drug.

At age thirty-six, Dr. Oscar Mentzer was buried in the prison cemetery.

DEATH BY GOLD FEVER

Note: In the interest of full disclosure, the victim in this case was the author's great-uncle.

In the year 1912, the quiet of a June morning in the hamlet of Ophir was marred by several gunshots. At the end of it, twenty-five-year-old Charles Turner lay in the dirt near the railroad tracks, blood pouring from his mouth and a hole in his chest. Standing over him with a .32-caliber pistol was forty-year-old Frank Ensign.

Born in Montreal, Charles Turner came with his family to Colorado in April 1884 at the age of five. His father, Decimus (Dess), took a job as a clerk at the early Denver department store of Charles Ballin & Company. He did not survive long in his new home. On October 30, 1886, Dess died of a sudden illness, leaving his wife, Agnes, on her own with four children, whose ages ranged from six to sixteen.

Over the next couple of years, Agnes (Brown) Turner was so stricken by her husband's death that she rarely left her bed. Once she recovered, she spent the next dozen or so years raising the four children as a single mother in frontier Denver. Although she had income from renting and later selling their property in Montreal, plus a possible death benefit from insurance, the family struggled to survive. She may have received help from several brothers who lived in Colorado; one ran a bakery in Denver and two others worked mining claims and ran the Brown Brothers construction company in Aspen, later moving to Telluride to become full-time miners.

The two older Turner sons, William and Newton, went to work as teenagers, starting out as "cash boys" and advancing on to positions such as

View of Ophir, Colorado. *Photo by Peter D. Turner.*

wrapper, clerk and inspector, mostly at the Daniels & Fisher dry goods store. The only daughter, Jessie, was fourteen when her father died, and she took on the job of caring for seven-year-old Charlie.

In 1895, Agnes was embroiled in a vicious lawsuit in Denver against a Denver businessman, to whom she had loaned or given for investment $4,000. He claimed he owed her nothing. She won her case, but it's not clear whether she ever collected the money.

In the late 1890s, when her children were grown, Agnes met and married Henry McGlothlin, a man about fifteen years her junior. Her two eldest sons left about that time—one returning to Canada and the other disappearing forever into unknown parts. Agnes, Charlie and Jessie all moved in 1904 with Henry to Pueblo, where the latter ran a water hauling company.

Meanwhile, Agnes's two brothers, Davy and John Brown of the Brown Brothers, had left Aspen and had taken up several mining claims near Telluride—on Mount Wilson, San Bernardo and Yellow Mountain. At some point, a third "brother" named Robert appeared on the scene. Newspapers noted that Robert was only twelve years old, however, so he may have been a cousin or perhaps an illegitimate son.

111

In early May 1899, a double tragedy struck the family when two of the Brown brothers died of pneumonia within a week of each other:

> *The JOURNAL a week ago today noted the death of John Brown, of Brown Brothers, at San Bernardo, and the serious illness of Robert, his brother, from the same disease. Sunday last Robert was taken to the hospital at Durango, where he died Thursday morning. So of these three sturdy Scotch brothers, only Davy remains. They owned and worked the Kendrick mine on the western point of Yellow mountain.*[131]

After the death of his brothers, Davy Brown stayed on in the region. At some point, he became partners with a man named Frank Ensign on six claims on Mount Wilson, near the Morning Star Mine. Ensign, by all accounts, was a hardworking man who had been in the area for some time. Formerly a compositor at the *Durango Democrat*, Frank had a brother, William Ensign, who was a well-known New York publisher. Frank was a hardy soul, well known and respected by the locals: "Frank Ensign, who came down from the Mayflower mine Saturday, went over to San Bernardo Sunday… Snow seems to have no terrors for Frank, for he was snowed up all winter at the Mayflower and could not get to town at all, and now as soon as he gets out at one place back he goes into another."[132]

When Charlie was in his early twenties, he moved to the San Juans to work as a miner. A few years later, in 1909, Davy Brown succumbed:

> *Old Davy Brown is dead. The news was received today by a telegram to C.M. [Charlie] Turner, employed by Manager J.L. Brown of the Buckeye Leasing company on the Butterfly Terrible from Mr. Turner's mother, who is a sister of the aged prospector so well known here.*
>
> *Davy's death occurred in Pueblo yesterday evening at the home of his sister, Mrs. McGlothlin and the cause of death was a hemorrhage of the brain.*
>
> *Mr. Brown owned some prospects and mining locations in the vicinity of Trout Lake.*
>
> *It was only a few weeks ago that he left Telluride for Pueblo. His death marks the passing of one of the land marks of this region and the old man (he was upwards of 70) will be remembered for many years by the friends he made while in this region.*[133]

Except when he was needed at home, Charlie stayed on. One newspaper notice says he worked at the Ames power plant. In 1910, he was listed in the

Charlie Turner (left). The man on the horse is probably his uncle, Davy Brown, whose mining claims lay at the root of the trouble. *Author's collection.*

The Brown brothers' cabin on Yellow Mountain, where Charlie Turner lived when he was shot. *Photo by Peter D. Turner.*

census at Trout Lake—probably living in the Brown brothers' cabin up on Yellow Mountain.

Agnes was named as the administratrix of Davy's estate and visited the area several times after his death, both on estate business and to visit Charlie. (Agnes stayed with her friends Mary and Con Meenan—Mary being the former Mary Mahoney, the wife of the "murdered" John Mahoney, supposedly killed by union strikers.)

The trouble began when, in 1911, Davy Brown's estate somehow fell into the hands of Frank Ensign. It's possible, based on Agnes's previous misadventures in handling money, that she declined or was unable to serve as administratrix of Davy's estate and Ensign was appointed to take over.

Charlie's feelings about Ensign and the family's financial situation are alluded to in this cryptic letter written from Pueblo to his brother, Newton Turner, who now lived in Ontario, Canada:

> *My dear Newton,*
> *Hope you old folks are well and everything going alright.*
> *Got a wire from Mann Monday saying he had instructed his broker to sell the bonds and haven't heard since. I got a little vexed and sent him a wire yesterday. Wire money immediately will stand no more persecution and signed Mother's name to it. I did it because H.L. can't stand this worry and of course Mother can't when she is worrying her.*
> *Oh never mind we will win out yet old fellow. Some day. I know we will cause I can't feel depressed.*
> *I only wish I had gone back in January when I intended going and Ensign wouldn't have allowed himself to be appointed for any amount of money and don't think anyone else would have. Mother was afraid of rheumatism though so here I am.*
> *Love to all, Charl*[134]

Although the identities of "Mann" and "H.L." are a mystery, the letter clearly indicates that Charlie was not pleased that Ensign had control of the estate and its mining claims.

The day after Charlie wrote the above letter, on August 24, 1911, Ensign published a notice in the *Telluride Journal* announcing the sale of Davy Brown's mining properties, nearly a dozen in total. Ensign had also been billing the estate during this period for ore assay services.

A short time later, Charlie Turner was back in Ophir, and over the next ten months, the relationship between the two disintegrated.

On the day of the shooting, Frank entered the small store in Ophir at about seven o'clock in the morning. There, he ran into Charlie, who confronted him. Frank was armed but Charlie was not. Nevertheless, Charlie followed him out of the store, threatening to "get" him. Frank drew his gun and said he would shoot if Charlie didn't leave him alone. Charlie kept coming. Frank fired at the ground. Charlie kept coming, and Frank fired off several more shots, hitting Charlie in the chest. Despite being shot, Charlie tackled Frank and had nearly wrestled the gun out of his hand when blood burst from Charlie's mouth and he fell over dead. He had been shot in the heart.

Sheriff Tallman soon arrived, along with Coroner Hadley and Dr. M.T. Rothwell. Tallman arrested Frank Ensign. Coroner Hadley held an inquest the following day. Several residents of Ophir testified that Charlie Turner was a troublesome fellow who had quarreled with several others in the village. Although just about everyone had been fond of Davy Brown and thought highly of Agnes, few had anything good to say about Charlie. Although Charlie was never mentioned in any of the numerous articles about Jesse Munn and his crime and subsequent months on the run—and despite the

View of Ophir in 1940. *Library of Congress, Prints & Photographs Division.*

Train tracks in Ophir where Charlie Turner was killed. *Drawing by Richard Turner.*

fact that Munn's friend Dick Martin was arrested for helping him escape—the *Telluride Journal* now claimed Charlie was involved:

> *According to Turner's own statement at the time of the Jesse Munn case he was the man who fed Munn and gave him a gun, assisting him to escape.*
> *According to reports from the Loop Turner has been mixed up in different scraps and fights around that place and boasted being a gun man and only about ten days ago walked up behind a man at the Loop and knocked him down and kicked him almost into insensibility.*[135]

Although the *Journal* painted Charlie as a crazed sociopath, the *San Miguel Examiner* was a bit more even-handed in summing up his character:

> *Turner was a fine looking, big six footer, who ought to weigh close to 200 pounds, and the man who shot him will not weigh to exceed 140 pounds. Turner had a bullying disposition and all that was bad in him in this respect seemed to crop out over there, although when we met him in Telluride he always seemed a perfect gentleman, and was so far as we were concerned.*[136]

After the inquest, Frank Ensign was set free. Charlie's body was sent to Agnes and Jessie in Pueblo, who took him to Denver and buried him in the Turner family plot at Riverside Cemetery.

In the years after Charlie's death, the newspapers noted several visits to Telluride by his sister, Jessie G. Turner. One family story says she spent an

This page: Ten months before he died, Charlie Turner wrote this letter to his nephew (the author's father) on the boy's second birthday. *Author's collection*.

entire winter by herself up at the Brown brothers' cabin. During one of these visits, she staked a claim on the property near the S.B. Kendrick Mine. Many years later, her nephew, Charles H. Turner (the author's father), found an old claim corner on the property. It was a rusted tobacco can containing a description of the property and Jessie Turner's name. On this property was the cabin where two of the "sturdy Scotch brothers" became fatally ill and where Charlie lived when he was shot. This land on Yellow Mountain was included in Frank Ensign's auction list as the one property that was held in fee, meaning Davy owned it free and clear. The property, called Matterhorn by descendants, reverted to the State of Colorado at some point. Years later, it was purchased for back taxes by the author's late father, Charles H. Turner, who, like the sturdy Scotch brothers and Frank Ensign and Uncle Charlie, suffered his entire life from gold fever.

NOTES

Wanted Dead or Alive: Jesse Munn

1. *San Miguel Examiner*, August 6, 1910.
2. *Telluride Journal*, August 4, 1910.
3. *Telluride Daily Journal*, April 24, 1909.
4. *Telluride Journal*, August 4 1910.
5. Ibid.
6. Ibid.
7. Ibid.
8. Ibid.
9. *San Miguel Examiner*, September 17, 1910.
10. *Ouray Plaindealer*, December 9, 1910.
11. *San Miguel Examiner*, December 10, 1910.
12. *Ouray Plaindealer*, December 9, 1910.
13. *Telluride Journal*, December 9, 1910.
14. Ibid.
15. Ibid.
16. *Telluride Daily Journal*, December 8, 1910.
17. Ibid.
18. Ibid.
19. *Ouray Plaindealer*, December 9, 1910.
20. Ibid.
21. *Telluride Daily Journal*, December 8, 1910.
22. *Telluride Daily Journal*, December 10, 1910.

23. Ibid.
24. Ibid.
25. *Ouray Herald*, December 16, 1910.
26. Ibid.
27. *Telluride Journal*, December 22, 1910.
28. *Ouray Plaindealer*, December 23, 1910.
29. *Telluride Journal*, January 5, 1911.
30. Ibid., March 16, 1911.

The Highgrader and Rattlesnake Liz

31. *San Miguel Examiner*, September 3, 1910.
32. Williamson, "Seven Ways to Compute the Relative Value of a U.S. Dollar Amount, 1790 to Present, Measuring Worth."
33. *San Miguel Examiner*, September 3, 1910.

The Troubled Saga of the Smuggler-Union Mine

34. Martin, *The Corpse on Boomerang Road*, 34.
35. *San Miguel Examiner*, April 27, 1901.
36. *Telluride Daily Journal*, June 29 1901.
37. Martin, *The Corpse on Boomerang Road*, 142.
38. *Telluride Daily Journal*, November 20, 1902.
39. Suggs, *Colorado's War on Militant Unionism*, 119–20.
40. Ibid., 121.
41. Ibid., 125.
42. Langdon, *Cripple Creek Strike*, 281–82.

The Snowy Adventures of the Millionaire Kid

43. *Telluride Daily Journal*, February 14, 1911.
44. Ibid., February 28, 1911.

WHERE IS JAMES O'KELLY?

45. *Silverton Standard*, May 23, 1908.
46. *San Miguel Examiner*, August 14, 1909.
47. Ibid., October 28, 1911.

SAN MIGUEL COUNTY BANK ROBBERY

48. Warner, *Last of the Bandit Riders*, 120–21.
49. Ibid., 121–22.
50. Ibid., 122.
51. Ibid., 123.
52. Ibid., 118.

THE LIFE AND TIMES OF THE TREMONT SALOON

53. *Telluride Daily Journal*, October 27, 1897.
54. Ibid.
55. Ibid., May 16, 1901.
56. Ibid., March 11, 1904.
57. Ibid., April 19, 1909.
58. Ibid., December 26, 1912.
59. Ibid., June 22, 1914.
60. Ibid., December 21, 1914.

THE DISAPPEARANCE OF A TOMBOY BRIDE

61. *Telluride Journal*, August 24, 1911.
62. Ibid., August 31, 1911.
63. *Telluride Daily Journal*, June 16, 1915.

BANQUETS AT THE TELLURIDE TREASURY

64. *San Miguel Examiner*, May 3, 1902.
65. *Ouray Herald*, May 9, 1902.

66. Williamson, "Seven Ways to Compute the Relative Value of a U.S. Dollar Amount, 1790 to Present, Measuring Worth."
67. *Telluride Daily Journal*, May 28, 1907.
68. *San Miguel Examiner*, June 1, 1907.
69. *Telluride Daily Journal*, May 28, 1907.
70. *San Miguel Examiner*, June 1, 1907
71. Williamson, "Seven Ways to Compute the Relative Value of a U.S. Dollar Amount, 1790 to Present, MeasuringWorth."
72. *San Miguel Examiner*, June 1, 1907.
73. *Telluride Daily Journal*, May 29, 1907.
74. Ibid.
75. Williamson, "Seven Ways to Compute the Relative Value of a U.S. Dollar Amount, 1790 to Present, Measuring Worth."
76. *Ouray Herald*, November 22, 1907.
77. *Telluride Daily Journal*, January 4, 1912.
78. *Telluride Journal*, April 18, 1912.

The Tale of the Trembling Bandit

79. *Telluride Journal*, August 31, 1911.
80. Ibid.

For Love of Diamonds

81. *Telluride Daily Journal*, September 9, 1921.
82. Ibid.
83. Ibid., November 15, 1921.
84. Ibid., October 24, 1921.
85. Ibid., November 16, 1921.
86. Ibid.
87. Ibid., November 22, 1921.
88. Ibid., December 30, 1921.

TELLURIDE'S GUNFIGHTER-DEPUTY, BOB MELDRUM

89. Walker, Wilkerson and Read, *Guilty...But Not as Charged*, 210.
90. Ibid., 128.
91. *Telluride Daily Journal*, November 23, 1903.
92. Ibid.
93. *Durango Democrat*, April 19, 1904.
94. *Ouray Plaindealer*, April 8, 1904.
95. *Telluride Daily Journal*, April 2, 1904.
96. Ibid., May 10, 1904
97. Ibid., April 4, 1904.
98. *Rawlins Republican*, April 13, 1904.
99. *Telluride Daily Journal*, January 18, 1912.
100. Ibid., November 6, 1908.
101. *Washington Post*, January 24, 1909.
102. *Sheridan Enterprise*, March 23, 1912.
103. *Cowley Progress*, August 8, 1913
104. *Rawlins Republican*, April 15, 1915.
105. *Rock Springs Miner*, July 1, 1916.

DOC MENTZER AND THE MYSTERIOUS MONROES

106. *Telluride Daily Journal*, October 11, 1898.
107. *San Miguel Examiner*, December 3, 1898.
108. *Telluride Daily Journal*, October 11, 1898.
109. *San Miguel Examiner*, October 8, 1898.
110. Ibid., December 3, 1898.
111. Williamson, "Seven Ways to Compute the Relative Value of a U.S. Dollar Amount, 1790 to Present, Measuring Worth."
112. *Telluride Daily Journal*, October 11, 1898.
113. Ibid., October 8, 1898.
114. Ibid.
115. *San Miguel Examiner*, October 8, 1898
116. *Telluride Daily Journal*, September 30, 1898; October 10, 1898.
117. *San Miguel Examiner*, October 8, 1898.
118. *Telluride Daily Journal*, October 11, 1898.
119. Ibid., October 12, 1898.

120. Ibid., October 18, 1898.

121. Ibid., November 22, 1898.

122. Ibid., December 2, 1898.

123. *San Miguel Examiner*, December 3, 1898.

124. Ibid.

125. *Telluride Daily Journal*, December 2, 1898.

126. Ibid., December 3, 1898.

127. Ibid., December 5, 1898

128. Ibid.

129. Ibid., December 8, 1898.

130. Ibid., December 12, 1898.

DEATH BY GOLD FEVER

131. *Telluride Daily Journal*, May 13, 1899.

132. *Telluride Journal,* June 27, 1907.

133. Ibid., March 4, 1909.

134. Letter from Charles Turner to Newton Turner, August 23, 1911.

135. *Telluride Daily Journal,* June 27, 1912.

136. *San Miguel Examiner,* June 29, 1911.

BIBLIOGRAPHY

BOOKS

Backus, Harriet Fish. *Tomboy Bride*. Boulder, CO: Pruett Publishing, 1980.

Barbour, Elizabeth, and the Telluride Historical Museum. *Images of America: Telluride*. Charleston, SC: Arcadia Publishing, 2006.

Buys, Christian J. *A Brief History of Telluride*. Lake City, CO: Western Reflections Publishing Company, 2007.

Churchill, E. Richard. *They Rode with Butch Cassidy: The McCartys*. Leadville, CO: Timberline Books, 1972.

Fetter, Richard L., and Susan C. Fetter. *Telluride: From Pick to Powder*. Caldwell, ID: Caxton Press, 1979.

Langdon, Emma F. *The Cripple Creek Strike: A History of Industrial Wars in Colorado 1903–4–5*. Denver, CO: Great Western Publishing Co., 1904–5.

Martin, MaryJoy. *The Corpse on Boomerang Road*. Montrose, CO: Western Reflections Publishing Company, 2004.

O'Neal, Bill. *Encyclopedia of Western Gunfighters*. Norman: University of Oklahoma Press, 1991.

Read, Marilyn, Ed Walker and Helen Wilkerson. *Guilty…But Not as Charged*. Denton, TX: Zone Press, 2009.

Suggs, George S., Jr. *Colorado's War on Militant Unionism*. Norman: University of Oklahoma Press, 1991.

Warner, Matt, as told to Murray E. King. *The Last of the Bandit Riders*. New York: Bonanza Books, 1940.

DOCUMENTS

Alfred A. Filby Appellant v. Agnes Turner. Colorado Court of Appeals. January
    1895. Colorado State Archives.

NEWSPAPERS

Cowley [WY] Progress
Durango [CO] Democrat
Ouray [CO] Herald
Ouray [CO] Plaindealer
Rawlins [WY] Republican
Rock Springs [WY] Miner
San Miguel Examiner [Telluride, CO]
Sheridan [WY] Enterprise
Silverton [CO] Standard
Telluride [CO] Daily Journal
Telluride [CO] Journal
Washington Post

WEBSITES

Williamson, Samuel H. "Seven Ways to Compute the Relative Value of a
    U.S. Dollar Amount, 1790 to Present, Measuring Worth." 2010. www.
    measuringworth.com/uscompare.

COLLECTIONS

Charles Turner Letters, 1911. Carol Turner Collection, Broomfield,
    Colorado.

ABOUT THE AUTHOR

C arol Turner was born and raised in Boulder, Colorado. Her roots go deep in frontier Colorado, with pioneer ancestors in Aspen, Pueblo, Denver and Telluride. Her great-grandmother's three brothers, fondly dubbed the "sturdy Scotch brothers," worked mining claims on Yellow Mountain, Mount Wilson, San Bernardo and other spots near Telluride in the 1890s and early 1900s. Her great-uncle, Charles M. Turner, was shot by a former partner over some of those mining claims in 1912 Ophir. Throughout the 1940s, '50s and '60s, her father, Charles H. Turner, was a mining engineer at several Colorado mines, including the Camp Bird Mine near Ouray.

Carol Turner has a BA in English from Sonoma State University and an MFA in creative writing and literature from Bennington College. She is the author of *Forgotten Heroes and Villains of Sand Creek*, *Notorious Jefferson County* and *Economics for the Impatient*. Her short fiction has appeared in numerous literary magazines. She lives in Colorado and writes a history column for the Broomfield Enterprise and a Colorado history blog. Visit her website at www.carol-turner-books.com.

Visit us at
www.historypress.net